DOGS IN BIRMINGHAM

Alton and Jo Douglas

© **1991 Alton & Jo Douglas**

ISBN 0 947731 83 0

Published by Brewin Books, Doric House, Church Street, Studley, Warwickshire B80 7LG
Printed by The Alden Press Ltd, Osney Mead, Oxford OX2 0EF

Individual training by Sandon Moss in Westley Road, Acocks Green, 1953.

FRONT COVER:
Actor Anthony Head with some of the dogs trained in the City, from Central TV's "Woof", 1991.

THE BIRMINGHAM DOGS' HOME

(A Company Limited by Guarantee, Registered in England, No. 662947)

MANAGER: J. D. GOODHEAD

Registered Office:

New Bartholomew Street, Birmingham B5 5QS. Tel: 021-643 5211

Appeals Office: Tel: 021-643 5018

Chairman:
W. S. ELLIS, MA. LL. M.

Secretary:
C. C. EVANS

Treasurer:
J. B. PRESCOTT
Lloyds Bank Plc,
9/11 Poplar Road,
Solihull,
West Midlands B91 3AN

Veterinary Director:
B. C. R. GRIFFITHS, B.Sc., M.R.C.V.S.
608 Warwick Road, Solihull,
West Midlands B91 1AA

Dear Friend,

Welcome to the wonderful world of dogs in Birmingham!

When Beryl Romano, Appeals Manager of the Birmingham Dogs' Home, asked us if we could produce a fund-raising book, Jo and I thought long and hard about the subject. We decided, rather than producing a book about the Home, that we would create a patchwork quilt of dog life in the city over the years, thereby giving it as much variety as possible. We felt it should show some evidence of how people viewed animals in the old days but that the emphasis, in the main, should be on the more recent past. It should pay tribute to a representative selection of other charities, contain a few well-known local people with canine connections, demonstrate the part that man's best friend has played in entertainment, fashion, work and advertising and so on. Wallow, if you will, in the sheer delight that our canine companions can conjure up with their stories of courage, devotion and love. Please remember that, with hundreds of breeds of dogs to choose from, there is no way we could possibly include them all — so we hope you'll enjoy our selection.

The Birmingham Dogs' Home, itself, was founded in 1892 for "Lost and Starving Dogs" and based in New Canal Street. The manager's house and kennels stayed on this site (with the addition of a puppy unit and a veterinary examination room in 1971) until 1988. Extensive blocks of kennels, a puppy unit, a cattery and a vet clinic were then built in New Bartholomew Street and officially opened by HRH, The Duchess of York, in September 1989. The financing comes from a wide variety of sources, such as slide shows, talks, boarding, donations and the selling of merchandise — including, of course, this book!

Thank you for caring.

MEMBER OF THE ASSOCIATION OF BRITISH DOGS HOMES (REGISTERED CHARITY No. 222436)

CONTENTS

From: Lieutenant Colonel Sean O'Dwyer

BUCKINGHAM PALACE

18th September, 1989

Dear Mr Ellis,

The Duchess of York has asked me to write and thank you for such an enjoyable visit to the Birmingham Dogs Home.

Her Royal Highness was most touched by your generous gifts of the brooch and the toy animal and has asked me to convey her sincere thanks and best wishes to you all.

Yours sincerely,

Sean O'Dwyer

W S Ellis Esq.

Three small Pomeranians, bred from Bournville Golden Legend (owned by Miriam and Ron Clay of Bournville) pop-up in Altoona, USA, 1960.

PUPPY LOVE

Bedtime Story

Birmingham Weekly Post

"A PRESENT FROM FAIRYLAND" 1945

IT was raining hard, and Joan sat sadly by the window watching the shining pools on the garden lawn. She was tired of playing by herself, and longed for the rain to stop so that she could go outside. "I do wish the sun would shine, and I do wish I had a playmate," she said, feeling very sorry for herself.

Almost before the last word was spoken there was a little chuckle just beside her, and looking down Joan saw a tiny little man. He was so small that she could hardly believe her eyes. "Let me introduce myself," said the little fellow. "My name is 'Happy,' and I've come to see why you're so unhappy." Joan was too surprised to say anything for a moment. Then, all in one breath, she said, "Oh! dear, I'm so lonely, and I can't go out to play because it's raining." The little man chuckled, and his face became wreathed in smiles. "Well! that is a pity," he said, "but things are only what you make them, you know, and if you'll look outside again, you'll see that the sun is shining beautifully." Sure enough, Joan saw that the sky was a lovely blue, and the garden was bathed in sunshine. It was a perfect summer's day. "There," said Happy, "you've just been looking at things the wrong way, you know. Come on, let's go outside."

Down they both ran on to the lawn. "I do wish I had a playmate, though," thought Joan, and just then Happy gave a short, sharp whistle. There was a patter of tiny paws, a flicker of black and white, and there, at Joan's feet, tugging at her shoe laces, was the sweetest, dearest little puppy she had ever seen. They romped and played together until they were breathless, and then Joan looked round for "Happy." The little man had quite disappeared.

"I feel quite tired," said Joan, and picking the puppy up in her arms, she ran indoors, and fell fast asleep on the seat by the window.

The next thing she knew was the rattle of tea-cups, and her mother telling her it was tea time. "Oh! Mummy," said Joan, "isn't it a lovely day. I've been playing in the garden with the loveliest little puppy." "You've been dreaming, dear," said her mother. "Why, it's been raining all the afternoon." "But, look, Mummy, here's the puppy on my lap." Sure enough, he was still there, a tightly-curled bundle of black and white. Joan's mother was very surprised, but in the matter-of-fact way that grown-ups have, she said, "He is a pretty little thing, dear. Perhaps he's a stray." "Oh! no, he's a present from Fairyland," said Joan. She smiled a secret little smile to herself, and whispered in the puppy's tiny ear, "I'll call you 'Happy,' to remind me of the little man who told me that things are only what you make them."

A quintet of Cavalier King Charles Spaniels, belonging to Eileen Brown, of Yardley Fields, 10th May 1961.

Zena and her seven-week-old family are a rare variety of Belgian Sheepdog, the Groenendael. Their owner is June Hemenway of Northfield, 29th August 1970. On the Continent, where they are not so rare, the breed was used by the Army during the war and many have been used as avalanche rescue dogs.

Mischief, owned by Estelle Wheels, proudly looks after her Dalmatian charges at Yardley, 22nd December 1971.

Time for the roll call

BEING a mother is a full-time job, particularly when, like Tess, the Bassett Hound, you have eight to keep in order.

Her puppies are four weeks old now and their capacity for mischief is exceeded only by their seemingly boundless energy.

It's not often she can get them all together in their basket for a roll-call: Diamond Lil, Norah, Spooky, Noirette, Dimity Star, Patch, and the boys, Callan and Lonely.

Don't humans choose some funny names? 16.5.72

DOING MY GOOD DEED.

I CAN'T KEEP IT IN ANY LONGER

I GOTTA SAY HELLO!

Puppy Class at the Sutton Coldfield Show, Kingstanding Community Centre, October 1971.

9

Pen pals together! Rough Collie pups, bred by Mary and Sid Jeys, enjoy the sunshine in Acocks Green, 1974.

9.12.75.

FIREWORK fun for five-year-old Jason Fenton is safe, warm and adorable. For in little Jason's own "box of fireworks" are nine cuddly Labrador puppies, each a five-week-old bundle of trouble.

They got their firework names because they were born on Guy Fawkes night. Now Jason, of Ontario Close, Kings Norton, Birmingham, has Rocket, Cracker, Catherine, Flash, Fireball, Comet, Flame, Explosion — and of course Guy — in hand.

Seven Golden Retrievers will soon leave their home in Sutton Coldfield to start careers all over the country as guide dogs, 10th December 1976.

Beagley, a Beagle pup, originally bred for research, instead became the pet of Carol and Christopher Wilde, of Northfield, 23rd December 1976.

Tascha, the Tibetan Terrier, at the home of the Hawkers in Hall Green, keeps an eye on Eddy, Piggy, Badger, Boots, Di, Foxy, Spot and Leo, 26th May 1977.

Pepe, the Toy Poodle, helps Sheba, the Red Setter, to look after her puppies at the home of Grace Davidson, Kings Norton, 28th September 1977.

Barry Littleford, of Weoley Castle, with Pom and Blue, his Hungarian Komondor puppies, 4th October 1977.

Candy, the Yorkshire Terrier, owned by Michelle Fisher, decides to check her weight, only to find that she's put on 2 pounds since she was born (20 weeks before weighing a mere 8 ounces) Erdington, 1982.

Former Crufts Best of Breed winning owner Doreen Dodd, of Erdington, has been named the leading Corgi breeder at the NEC, 24th January 1983.

Oscar, owned by Gill du Cros, has had a very successful first year in the show ring with several wins, including Best Puppy Dog at the Birmingham Doberman Club Open Show, Great Barr Leisure Centre, May 1991.

A football team of English Bull Terriers, proudly displayed by Alan Bearman, 15th March 1989. Harborne was the arrival spot for these daughters and sons of Cher.

"Do you know that your dog bit
mother-in-law yesterday?"
"No; is that so? Well, I suppose
will sue me for damages?"
"Not at all. What will you take
the dog?"

BIRMINGHAM DOGS
HOME - PUPPY HOUSE

FERGIE OPENS
NEW DOGS HOME

Colin Whittock.

"- I CAN'T UNDERSTAND IT, SHE TOOK ONE LOOK AT ME AND WENT PALE...!"

CARE OF THE DOG

1923

CHAINED-UP DOGS. 1911

Some dogs have more care and affection lavished upon them than firstborn babies, and others are treated with such indifference that we are delighted when their owners are prosecuted for their cruelty. I heard a few days ago of a man who kept a dog almost constantly chained up, making him go weeks at a time between short spells of freedom. Naturally, the condition of the dog became extremely filthy, and its wailing was loud and pitiable beyond endurance. At last a neighbour intervened, and threatened an immediate prosecution if the poor animal were not destroyed in his presence. This the heartless owner assented to and the matter dropped.

Of course, it is not possible for every dog-owner to give his dog unlimited freedom, and there are some who have little opportunity of affording the exercise of a walk. It may well be argued that such people have no business to keep a dog, and if only those who can spare reasonable time and proper attention kept pets much needless misery would be saved. But human nature is a curious mixture, and we have to make the best of it.

Those who "must" keep a dog even though they have not much time to devote to it, and are therefore obliged to keep it chained up for long periods at a time, should take note of the excellent idea depicted in the little sketch. A stout wire is securely fixed from a point close to the kennel to some point twenty yards or so distant. To a ring on this wire the dog's chain is attached with

WIDE RUN FOR CHAINED-UP DOGS.

a swivel to allow for his innumerable gyrations. This will permit of a good long run, which though far from being as good as unrestricted liberty is sufficient to keep the dog fairly happy and healthy. Of course, the wire has to be arranged so as not to inconvenience those who approach the house on legitimate business, but it can be fixed so as to give the dog an extensive patrol of the property at night-time, to the great embarrassment of intruders.

Over-feeding

"THE British love of a dog is something quite inexplicable. In these days, except to a shepherd, dogs are animals of little practical use, but their lives and well-being seem to be almost as important as those of human beings.

"Any veterinary surgeon can tell you a woman's dog immediately it walks into his sight. It is always too fat, as a result of over-feeding and coddling. Women are too kind-hearted and maternal; they kill their dogs with kindness.

1942

MOST little children love animals, and if accustomed to them from their earliest years very seldom have any fear of them. If it is at all possible, it is a good plan to give a child a pet—a dog, a cat, a bird, some rabbits and let it look after it. The child must be taught to make its pet comfortable, see that it gets food and water, etc. This need for thoughtfulness for dumb animals is all valuable training. The child who possesses and loves a pet of its own will not be inclined to tease or be unkind to any animal later on in life.

DOGS AND THEIR OWNERS.

1926

PRACTICAL FEEDING.

Need for Balanced Rations.

By A. CROXTON SMITH.

Theory cannot be divorced from practice when we are endeavouring to construct a correctly-balanced ration for any class of domestic animal. One is supplementary to the other.

Science, having produced the ideas, proceeds to ascertain how they will work. Sometimes they do not function, in which case the investigator has to go over the ground again until his experiments are crowned with success.

I was much struck with a remark made by Professor T. B. Wood in a paper on rations for normal animals, read before a meeting of the National Veterinary Medical Association at Cambridge. He suggested that the proteins of any ration should be derived from different sources, because proteins differ very markedly from one another in composition.

One of the speakers, in discussing the paper, also remarked that a certain mixture, although theoretically a good milking ration, causes digestive disturbances, which send a cow off her head, with the result that there is hardly any milk.

Obviously, a ration blended in strictly scientific proportions is not always satisfactory.

CORRECT MIXING.

The test of any theory is in its application. No matter how correct a mixture may be in the quantity of its constituents, it will not commend itself to practical men unless it does what it professes to do. The able scientist experiments as well as originates.

Some day we shall realise that every farmer will be compelled to seek the assistance of the scientist, because proper feeding is also economical feeding. An ill-balanced ration is an expensive luxury.

Fortunately, the average dog-owner does not have to worry himself much about these matters, the manufacturers of biscuits and meals producing foodstuffs that have passed the test of experience satisfactorily.

During the build-up to the Second World War one of the major fears was that the enemy would use gas against the civilian population. This was one of the types of gas-proof dog kennels that were invented at the time, 7th December 1938.

TO THE RESCUE OF A FAITHFUL FRIEND IN DISTRESS

PDSA, Islington Row, 26th July 1957. The PDSA also had premises in Soho Hill, Handsworth and Lichfield Road, Aston.

Roxy supervises the eating arrangements for her Golden Retriever pups at Bob Powell's home, Hall Green, 1959.

Not enough dogs in home to go round

1971

Evening Mail Reporter

SO many dogs left Birmingham Dogs' Home last week with new owners that some people who went there for pets left disappointed.

Mr. John Goodhead, manager of the home, said that 170 dogs that were to have been destroyed had been found homes during the week.

But he appealed today to people who went away empty handed at the weekend to call again. He said: "Hundreds of dogs will be coming to us."

BUSIEST

He said last week was one of the busiest on record for the home, in New Canal Street.

Nobody would think I was supposed to be looking after this puppy!

BUT WE ARE GOOD PALS REALLY

MICKEY the monkey is bringing up a baby poodle!

At its Billesley home, in Trittiford Road, its owner, Mrs. Jean Clewer, said: "They say monkeys will have nothing to do with dogs, but we can't keep Mickey away from the poodles."

Mickey's special pet is three-weeks-old Solitaire who he took to at its birth.

"When he saw it," explained Mrs. Clewer "he curled his tail around it, and that was it—it was his baby."

Carried

Mickey, who is a year old, washes Solitaire, and carries it around between his legs.

Said Mrs. Clewer: "First thing in the morning he makes straight for the dining room to see where it is, and sits and eats his breakfast with him.

"At night, when we say 'bed' Mickey looks at Solitaire, and would take him to bed, but we don't let him."

Unbelievable

Mrs. Clewer, who runs a poodle parlour at her home, bought Mickey from a friend five months ago. The friend warned her: "Keep him away from dogs."

But Mickey plays with the eight other poodles at Mrs. Clewer's home, and has confounded the vet, who "cannot believe he is so good with dogs."

He rides on the poodles' backs, and is fond of Mrs. Clewer's cat.

Bother this De Gaulle bus --snap out of it and come walk."

14

The pupils at Yorke House Preparatory School, Hall Green, are involved in a course of pet care. Katie, the Pekingese, does her own bit of caring by giving a pick-a-back ride to a guinea pig, 1964.

Dog-lover, Alan Hutchinson, starts his new job as a dog warden, 4th February 1978. Here the former police dog instructor poses with a neighbour's Corgi – one animal that won't cause him any problems!

A variation on the theme of "Walkies" is tested by a volunteer, 1978. The inventor, Hiroshi Kawasaki, watches as Mark gingerly takes his first steps.

Great Danes, Zeus and Tiger, are eating their way through a mound of food at the RSPCA Kennels in Barnes Hill, July 1982.

16

BIRMINGHAM DOGS HOME

PET SERVICE

SERVICE OF THANKSGIVING

SUNDAY 1st OCT. 1989

AT 3·00 P.M.
AT

St. AUGUSTINES CHURCH
LYTTELTON ROAD. EDGBASTON.
(NEAR NORFOLK HOTEL)

COME ALONG,
BRING YOUR PET.

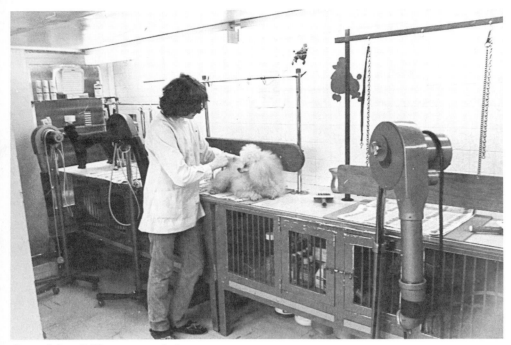

AFTERNOON TEA.

Josephine Dillon at work in the clipping room of the Chafirlock Poodle Parlour, Billesley, c. 1980.

JUST A THOUGHT
Pal

ALL evening you have slumbered at my feet beside the chair, and while I worked I found great comfort knowing you were there. A sense of rare companionship was in the atmosphere—the ease of perfect silence as with friends who are sincere. Preoccupied, my hand might stray to smooth your coat so sleek and you would thump your tail but never interrupt or speak. And then those velvet eyes would blink and patiently you'd wait till I observed your evening walk was quite an hour late.

—KATHLEEN PARTRIDGE

Chibbi, the Chihuahua, relaxes in a four-poster bed, just one of the luxury items available for pets this Christmas, December 1987.

Problems with a paw? Attention is given at the PDSA veterinary centre, Grosvenor Road, Aston, 1990.

HEEL!

Sandon Moss, President of Solihull Dog Training Club, at work, c. 1954. The Club, at Billesley Community Centre, Yardley Wood, apart from its obedience tuition, raises money for all types of charities, canine and otherwise.

19

"NOT A FIGHTING DOG" 1952

THERE ARE still quite a number of people who are, prejudiced against Staffordshire Bull Terriers, because of what these dogs were originally bred for fighting. The continued reference to the breed as "fighting dogs," however, should be stopped immediately because it is doing a certain amount of harm. There is no doubt that against any opposition at his weight the Stafford could, and would, give a good account of himself, but let it be understood first and foremost that he also has brains. He is a highly intelligent animal (usually reaching his peak form at eighteen months of age) and therefore easily taught to be obedient, without showing any lack of spirit. A lot of people fail to realise this, including some of our specialist judges. Why I mention some judges is because of their reference in show reports of certain exhibits showing or lacking the desired spirit. Maybe one of them will be kind enough to inform me how he knows when an exhibit shows this desired spirit. By continual barking, snarling, etc. ? I have proved to my own satisfaction that these displays simply convey the particular Stafford's dislike to his company.

BEWARE
UNPREDICTABLE OWNERS & ECCENTRIC DOGS

PLEASE PLEASE SHUT THE GATE

Despite the arctic conditions the training has to go on, 1956.

Part of the Birmingham Dog Training Club Show line-up at the New Inn, Coventry Road, Sheldon, 1957.

Kurt, the German Short-Haired Pointer, waits for his next command, Kings Norton, 1966. Shirley Robinson uses him for the training of obedience and agility.

Afghan training

A CLUB formed to train Afghan hounds holds its first meeting in Birmingham next Tuesday.

"We are told that we are the first club of its kind," says Mrs. Carole Addis, of 31 St. Martin's Avenue, Priory Fields, Studley.

"Afghans are a breed of dog rapidly growing in popularity . . . but although they have lovely natures, they are difficult to train.

"That is because it is only in the last 100 years that man has brought them in to live with him.

"Up to then, they were semi-wild herding dogs — as many still are in their native mountains.

"Although they are gentle, they are hard to get back once they are off the lead, so we owners have tried taking them to dog training classes for all breeds.

"This has not been a success, so we have formed a specialist Birmingham Afghan training club, with Kennel Club permission.

"Experts will be coming from many parts of the country to help.

"The first meeting will be at the Saracen's Head, at King's Norton.

"Inside, naturally. Then there can be no difficulty in getting the dogs back. But we may try to hire a field as training progresses."

Nov 1971

20

SUTTON COLDFIELD AND DISTRICT DOG TRAINING CLUB

1991

VENUE: SUTTON UNITED FOOTBALL GROUND
HOLLYFIELD ROAD, SUTTON COLDFIELD

"THIS DOG"

I once sat in the vet's and listened to a man boasting for half an hour about how clever and obedient "THIS dog" of his was. The vet came in, called out the man's name, and as he stood up the puppy bit his owner! This is roughly how the boasting went :

THIS dog's taught himself to whistle,
Bark and then come running in.
THIS dog fills his bowl with water
And unscrews his biscuit tin.
THIS dog takes himself for walks
And even shops around for meat.
THIS dog's got his act together -
THIS dog's made me obsolete.

A.D.

"Is your dog intelligent?"
"Very. When I say to him, 'Come here or don't come here, just as you please,' he comes or he doesn't come, as he pleases."

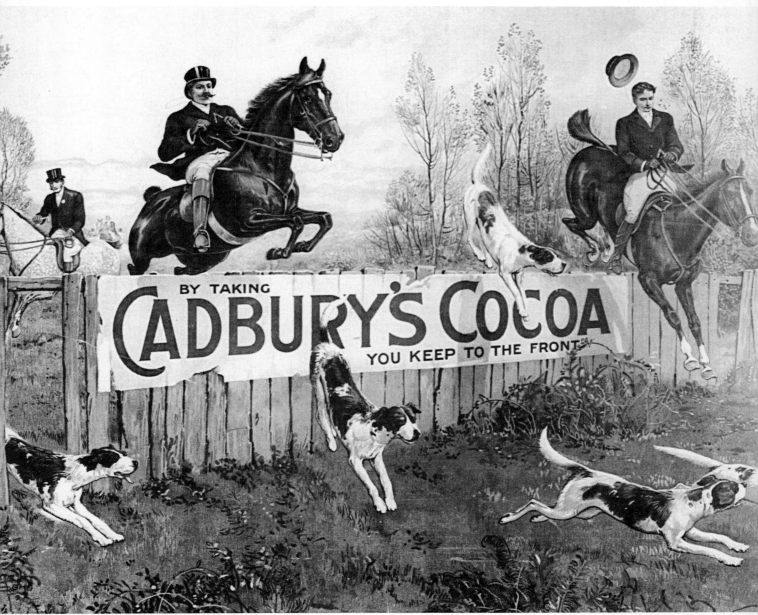

" FRIENDS SAY he's a credit to me

*B*UT credit is due to ALL-in-ONE, too. It keeps him in superb condition, because it contains all the essentials for perfect canine fitness. He enjoys every meal of it: its delicious 'meatiness' never loses its attraction."

ALL-in-ONE is sold by Corn Merchants, Grocers, etc., in 4½d. and 9d. cartons, 6d. and 1/- bags, and loose at 4½d. per lb. If your dealer does not stock, please send 4½d. in stamps, and you will receive a 4½d. carton of ALL-in-ONE Kennel Meal, together with a trial supply of MORSELS, the small, crunchy bone-shaped dog biscuits, and a copy of the interesting and informative booklet "About your dog." Please mention the name and address of your Dealer when writing.

Start your dog now on—
ENTWISTLES 1936
ALL-IN-ONE
KENNEL MEAL

A mealtime treat for your dog

ENTWISTLES LTD., (Dept. R.T.), Vulcan St. Mills, Liverpool 3.

164 PAGES 2D

Everyone who owns a dog should also own this famous book. Written by a leading veterinary surgeon, it is a complete guide to the care of dogs in health and sickness. Deals with feeding, breeding, showing, ailments, accidents and everything you want to know about your dog. A host of illustrations and coloured plates.

Amazing bargain. 2d. from chemists, stores and corn merchants. 1937

'Happy spirits, lovely coat, keen appetite—every sign of doggy fitness depends on a pure bloodstream. Your dog too will always enjoy this sparkling condition if you purify his blood with 'one Bob Martin's once a day.'

In packets 9 for 7d. 36 for 1/11 1944
BOB MARTIN'S

He looks to you for his
spring conditioning
1938

NOW is the time to condition your dog— to cleanse his blood of all the impurities which have collected as the result of richer feeding and lack of exercise during the winter. If you neglect to help him now, the first spell of warm weather will aggravate these impurities and lead to a succession of miserable blood disorders, such as continual scratching, listlessness, loss of appetite, loose coat and eczema, and swellings between the toes.

All he needs is a spring-conditioning course of Bob Martin's Condition Powders, which contain the natural blood correctives that a dog in his wild state would find for himself in certain herbs and grasses. For forty-five years experienced people have given their dogs this springtime course—three Bob Martin's a day for a week. Don't risk your dog's health any longer. **Every day as the sun grows warmer, his danger becomes greater.** Get a packet of Bob Martin's NOW. You can get them for 6d. and 1/- from all chemists and dog shops

Bob Martin's
CONDITION POWDERS
for better health, better coat, better spirits

WITH A GOOD HEART

Carol Hunt, from Bordesley Green, puts Beretta, the Dalmatian, in a sitting position, and collects cash for every minute he stays there, up to a maximum of ten, 27th August 1978. All monies raised will be used to ensure that every dog on their arrival at the Birmingham Dogs' Home is injected against diseases, such as distemper.

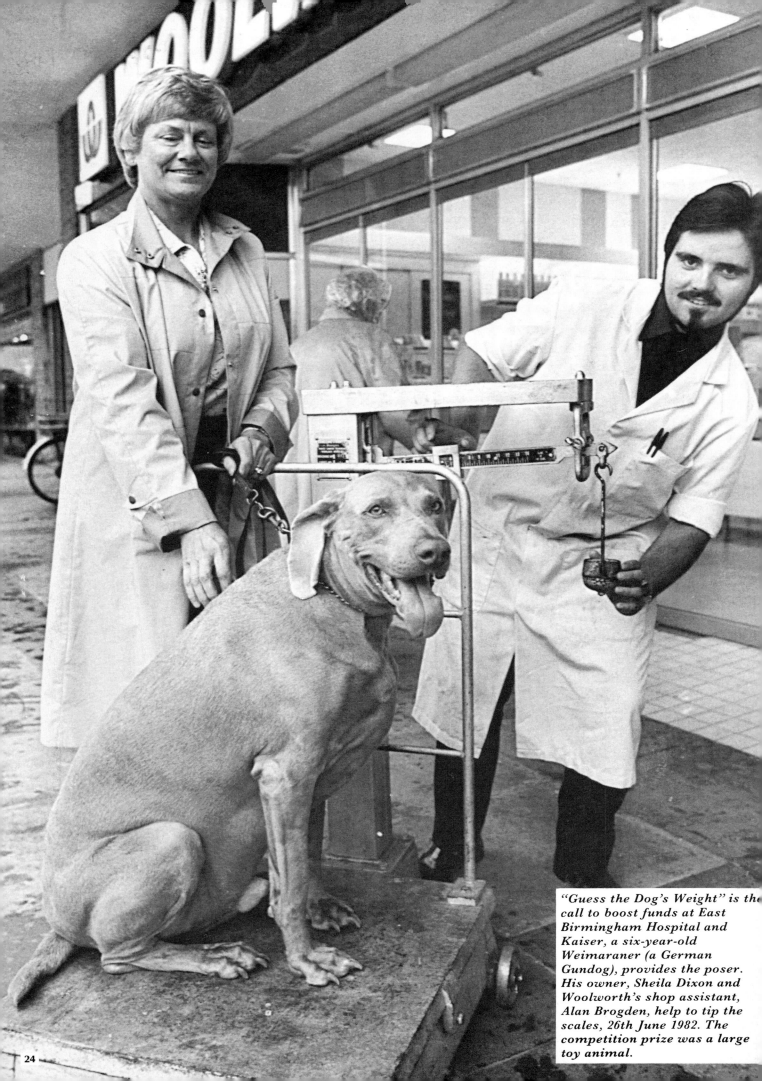

"Guess the Dog's Weight" is the call to boost funds at East Birmingham Hospital and Kaiser, a six-year-old Weimaraner (a German Gundog), provides the poser. His owner, Sheila Dixon and Woolworth's shop assistant, Alan Brogden, help to tip the scales, 26th June 1982. The competition prize was a large toy animal.

The Lord Mayor and Lady Mayoress, Coun. Peter Hollingworth and his wife, Patricia, visit the recently-opened PDSA centre in Grosvenor Road, Aston, 1982.

A GOOD TONIC

With a dog for my companion and a pathway
    with a view,
Every leafy haunt becomes a treasure hunt
    for two,
Each bend a great adventure, every flower
    a fragrant prize,
Each shadow the reflection of a blessing in
    disguise.

The blowing leaves are playmates that we
    two can scamper after,
And every sunbeam dancing holds a new
    excuse for laughter.
Could there be a better tonic than a romp
    to cure a frown,
With a dog for my companion and a road
    that leads from town.

                                        Kathleen Partridge.

PRO·DOGS

'PRO DOGS CARES, AND IT'S CARING THAT COUNTS'

THE P.D.S.A.

25

Just a walk for their friends

Taking the dog for an afternoon stroll helped to raise about £3,000 for less fortunate canine friends.

The sponsored two-mile walk in Pype Hayes Park, Erdington, was held to collect cash for the restoration work appeal at Birmingham Dog's Home.

And some of the famous faces among the 2,000 who took part, included Crossroads star Sue Hanson (Miss Diane), her husband, pop star Carl Wayne, Alton Douglas, Colin Gibson of Aston Villa and the Deputy Lord Mayor of Birmingham, Councillor Peter Hollingsworth with his wife, Patricia.

Ladies' hairdresser Miss Margaret Row, organised the day after she successfully ran a similar venture last year.

"I wanted to beat last year's total of £1,663, and I think I will have done that easily if all the sponsorship money comes in," she said.

"We raised about £1,000 from the stalls and shows along. It was a marvellous day."

The restoration appeal hopes to raise £400,00 in four years.

23.6.83

TV Weatherman, Alan Brown, takes part in the proceedings at the Birmingham Dogs' Home Summer Fun Day, Pype Hayes Park, Erdington, June 1984.

It is walkies with a difference for Mr Mark McDermott and his dog, Bengi, taking part in the RSPCA sponsored walk in Sutton Park, Birmingham. Mr McDermott, a chef at Penns Hall Hotel, Sutton Coldfield, believes in walking tall to raise money for a £40,000 animal welfare clinic and is no stranger to stilts, having used them before on charity walks. 6.7.85

Dachshund–Half a dog high by a dog and a half long.

Hot dog Sophie, the Dachshund, from Castle Vale, takes part in the RSPCA walk through Sutton Park, 6th July 1985.

Tina Bramwell, with her pets Sheba and Roma, 28th June 1985. A pupil of Whitesmore School, Chelmsley Wood, Tina is a great fund-raiser for animal charities.

Noel Blackham and his six-year-old, Monique, walked from John O'Groats to Land's End – a journey of 870 miles from 13th April to 24th May 1988 (despite a week off for attention to the cross-Collie's paw). Just one more example of the unselfish fund-raising that goes on for so many charities (this time the Birmingham Dogs' Home benefited).

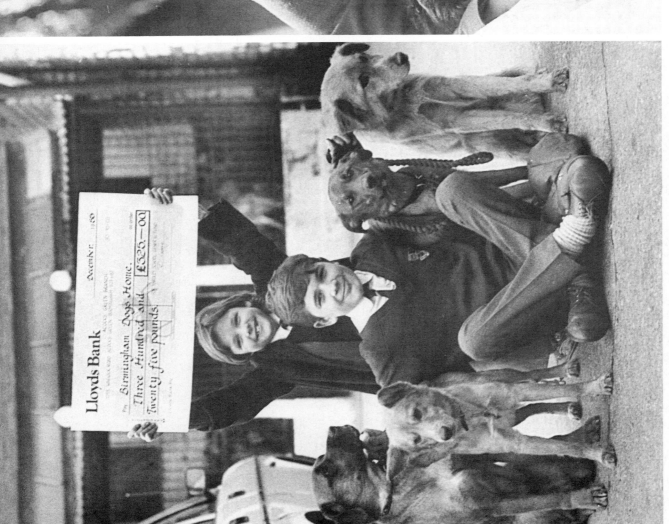

Teenagers from Yardley Middle School held car washes, can collections, sponsored events, and even a mini-Crufts to raise money to buy a kennel and bed for the Birmingham Dogs' Home. Christopher Flavell and Julie Rogers present a cheque for £325, 10th December 1985.

Staff at Tyseley electrical firm, MEM, raised money by collecting coppers for eight months and then holding a competition to guess how much the pile was worth. Dora Bryan, starring in the Hippodrome's production of "Charlie Girl", presents a cheque for £326 to Walter Kinder, of the Guide Dogs for the Blind Association, 15th January, 1980.

30

BUPA employees gather around a picture of their adopted dog, Bonny, after raising £1,000 to train her as a guide dog, 31st May 1988. The staff, from Vicarage Road, Edgbaston, raised the money from a combination of raffles, lotteries and pub crawls.

As part of the Pat Dog scheme Diane Smith takes her cross-Collie, Prince, to meet Frances Tisley and Nellie Perks at Lyttleton House, Frankley, July 1991.

The City of Birmingham Leo Club presents a cheque to Hearing Dogs for the Deaf, High Hall, Edgbaston, 1989.

DOGS FOR THE DISABLED

32

WORK 'N DOGS

1904

DOGS & THEIR OWNERS.

The RETRIEVER: "Dear me, he's getting quite to walk as I do, and he holds his head very much as I do also."

Get Your Dog to Help You

THE dog is an affectionate and loyal companion to man. It was probably the first of the animals to be domesticated and from prehistoric times to the present it has served man faithfully as a companion and guardian of himself and his property.

But seeing how intelligent dogs are, it is rather curious that more has not been done to train them to do useful work. Of course, the lady or girl with a lap-dog and the man or boy with a terrier teaches the pet to do certain tricks, such as begging for sugar, catching a ball, and so on, but these are merely interesting feats and not useful.

Why should not dogs generally be taught to do things that are really useful? Now and again one sees a dog going down to the newsagent's to fetch the morning paper; occasionally a dog is seen carrying a parcel or even fetching the milk, but these instances are rare.

That the dog is quite capable of doing really good work, almost human in its cleverness, is proved by the use to which it is put in the rounding up of sheep. Anyone who has watched on its hind legs, catches hold of the rope, and rings the bell as well as a human being could do.

The other instance of intelligence and cleverness in a dog is that of an animal belonging to Captain Cole, the pier-master at Weston-super-Mare. This animal seems to know every word his master says, and when the order is given the animal goes to the flag mast and actually hoists the Union Jack.

At another command it will ring the bell that warns passengers that their steamer is about to leave. Not only does it perform these feats regularly, but on instruction it will go to the beach and haul in a rowing boat used by the employees of the pier. This animal, Jack by name, is a wire-haired terrier, and it is certainly very intelligent and a great friend of all those who know it.

There is no reason why people who have dogs and will take a little trouble should not get them to do little jobs of this kind. Any simple task that needs doing regularly at a certain hour can be carried out by an intelligent dog.

1930

NATIONAL CANINE DEFENCE LEAGUE

ZEE CODE BOGIE BOI—Fee £5 5s. The famous Sire of many winners, and charming Miniatures including the Pair purchased by H. H. Maharaja of Jind, also the 2 and 3lb. Miniatures greatly admired at Crufts.

ZEE CODE MUTZEE Red. Fee £4 4s. Equally as good. Both well known winners including Best in Show (all Breeds) others from £2 2s. First Prize Winners.

Mrs. M. A. MORSE,

"The Bungalow," Lincoln Road, Acocks Green. Birmingham.

1929

19th August.—A research unit at B'ham Accident Hospital is seeking ways and means of making textiles non-inflammable. It has been estimated that two-thirds of all serious burns are due to clothes catching fire.

20th August. The B'ham City Council delegation of eight members led by the Lord Mayor, flying to Sverdlovsk, broke their 2,600 mile journey at Moscow and in the words of the Lord Mayor of Birmingham, were accorded a very warm welcome. The party spent a busy day in sight-seeing in Moscow, and was entertained to luncheon by the chairman of the executive council of the Moscow Soviet, Mr. M. A. Yasnov.

21st August.—Dogs are used at a building site in Staplelodge Road, West Heath, to keep away pilferers when workmen are absent. Previously there had been many losses. A demonstration was given to-day of the way in which a boxer dog can respond to training.

22nd August.—The B'ham Municipal Party made a tour of Sverdlovsk to-day. Messages of goodwill were presented and expressed the hope that the visit would consolidate friendly ties between the two peoples.

23rd August. A twin-jet Canberra bomber crossed the Atlantic twice to-day making the round trip in 14 hours, 21 minutes, 45 seconds, including a 35 minute refuelling stop in New York. The average speed was 481.52 m.p.h.
A warm day in B'ham was followed by the hottest night since 1950.

24th August.—Known in the underworld of B'ham as the "Ghost Squad," the police Crime Squad have achieved great success as trackers and breakers of criminal gangs since it was formed as a special branch in February, 1952.

1956

A family moved from the city to the suburbs, and were told they ought to get a watchdog to guard the premises at night. So they bought the largest dog that was for sale in the kennels of a near-by dealer.

Shortly afterwards the house was entered by burglars, who made a good haul while the dog slept. The householder went to the dealer and told him about it.

"Well, what you need now," said the dealer, "is a little dog to wake up the big dog!"

As an extra security measure a round-the-clock radio link is provided for Police dog handlers inside the grounds of Winson Green Prison, 14th March 1960.

Corporal J. Barrie, of Bordesley Green and Air Dog Rusty, 19th May 1962.

Sultan, the guard dog who will guard dogs because of the danger of their being doped or stolen, is recruited at Perry Barr greyhound track, 17th December 1970. His owner is security guard Bill Roberts, of Erdington. Perry Barr opened in 1928.

Inspector John Howell instructs prison officers from Winson Green, 19th February 1968. (Left to right) Ken Oliver with Simba, Derek Hall with Rebel and Michael Ness with King.

35

FIONN, the famous wolfhound mascot of the Irish Guards, gave rides to children when he visited a Bir-

Miss Mary Kelly, who presented a bouquet to the Lady Mayoress, meeting Fionn and his handler, Lance Corporal Robert O'Toole. Looking on are, left to right, Colonel J. A. Aylmer (Regimental Lieutenant-Colonel), the Lord Mayor and Lady Mayoress, and Major-General W. G. S. Mills (General Officer Commanding, West Midland District). 1970

11.3.74.

BRIAN Boru turned up to see the Lord Mayor of Birmingham today, nursing a bit of a hangover . . . and Brian is only four years old. But despite drinking four pints of a well-known Irish stout last night, Brian showed no sign of it when he was presented to the Lord Mayor, Councillor Mrs. Marjorie Brown, at the Council House.

And he even had enough energy to down another pint of stout offered to him by the Lord Mayor.

Brian is an Irish Wolfhound and regimental mascot of the Second Battalion of the Royal Irish Rangers, based at Warminster.

He joined the Army as a puppy

How did you get so many stripes—wouldn't you take a commission?"

"Yes," the teacher explained, "quite a number of plants and flowers have the prefix 'dog.' For instance, the dog rose and the dog-violet are well-known. Can you name another?"

There was silence, then a happy look illuminated the face of a boy at the end of the class.

"Please, Miss," he called out, proud of his knowledge, "collie-flowers."

Laddie, a Birmingham Post and Mail newsvendor's dog, rests at his pitch, Queensway Circus, 4th June 1982.

When the Austin Terrier Truck was launched, in 1971, some of the promotional material was packed inside cans, which were made to look like tins of dog food. Fergie, the Wire-Haired Terrier, owned by Yvette Braddock, was the model used on the labels.

Paula Pugh greets Noble and his handler, Pc George Russell, 3rd April 1981. Children from Victoria School for the Physically and Mentally Handicapped in Northfield monitored Noble's progress after he joined the police force by weighing and measuring him and watching his training.

Pc Robert Woodall and his dog, Max, make friends with fourth-year pupils from Perry Common School, College Road, Erdington, 19th July 1988. The youngsters were studying law and order as part of their B-Tech course.

The Dulux dog and Miss England, Tracey Williams, open the refurbished W. H. Smith Do-It-All Store in Stirchley,
30th November 1988. Brian Rose, of Selly Oak, offers a bit of his chocolate bar to the Old English Sheepdog.

Ivor, one of the "workers" for Dogs for the Disabled, 1991. The organisation provides trained animals for companionship, exercise motivation and to carry out certain household chores.

Pc Mick Brockley with Zeb (the Spaniel) and Pc Bob Hopcutt with Barney (the Alsatian), enjoy a moments break outside the Council House before preparing to take part in the West Midlands Police Open Day, 20th June 1989. Zeb is one of the dogs used for sniffing jobs, such as looking for drugs.

Guide dog Yana, is now a full card-carrying member of the Banking Insurance and Finance Union. Her owner, Mrs Sylvia Beese, works as a telephonist at the National Westminster's Bennetts Hill branch. They are seen here with Mrs Ann Bromwich (left) during the presentation at the bank, 5th October 1983.

The West Midlands' first civilian working trials champion, Molto, and his handler, Bill Stokes, of Great Barr, 31st August 1984. His wins at Dundee and Hampshire included honours for working dog, utility dog, companion and tracker.

Judith Moore, confined to her wheelchair with multiple sclerosis, was forced to stay indoors, in Edgbaston, when Gemmia outgrew her pulling harness. Now thanks to a special harness provided by the West Midlands Task Force Ltd, of Great Barr the pair are back on their travels again, 7th December 1983.

Kate Foye and Fandango prepare to spread a little sunshine, 28th February 1984. The Kerry Blue is the first of the City's "Pat Dogs" (a scheme whereby friendly canines visit the sick and elderly to cheer them up).

Rob, fourth in the recent contest at the Tally Ho Police training centre, once went missing for four months. He was finally spotted by handler Pc Malcolm Bryan's wife wandering with a pack of dogs in Nechells. March 1987.

IN FASHION

Wendy Wood with Wellington.

42   *Jayne Minchella with Milly.*

Gillian Flower with Leila.

CATALOGUE

OF THE

NATIONAL EXHIBITION

OF

SPORTING AND OTHER

DOGS,

HELD AT

The Midland Counties Repository,

CHEAPSIDE, BIRMINGHAM,

ON

MONDAY & TUESDAY, DECEMBER 3RD & 4TH.

BIRMINGHAM:
PRINTED BY M. BILLING, LIVERY STREET.

Prize poultry and dogs at the Birmingham Show, 1871.

1865.

CATALOGUE

OF THE

SIXTH

GREAT ANNUAL EXHIBITION

OF

Sporting and other Dogs,

WHICH WILL BE HELD IN THE

CURZON EXHIBITION HALL,

BIRMINGHAM,

ON

MONDAY, TUESDAY, WEDNESDAY, AND THURSDAY,

DECEMBER 4th, 5th, 6th, and 7th, 1865.

M. BILLING, SON, & CO, Printers, Livery Street, Birmingham.

...he electric light has been a great success at ... Dog Show. Why won't Mr. Chamberlain ... us one or two in "Municipal Square?" It ...uld make such a difference, and then we could ... that fine "arrangement in gold" over the ...n entrance.   1878

If you have a dog and require a name for it, don't call it "Chamberlain," because it will be a direct insult on the Member for West Birmingham. If you should call it "Kruger," you would be insulting the dog.
1901

A FREAK OF THE CAMERA

IT used to be said that the camera cannot
lie, but it can certainly give some very
curious effects.

In the picture on this page a lady was
photographed at a dog show with her exhibit,

NOT A STUDIO PHOTOGRAPH

and the result was certainly not what had
been anticipated.

The picture gives a very good photograph of
the dog, but it can hardly be called a good
portrait of the lady !

1929

THE annual show of the Midland Fox Terrier Club opened yesterday
at Curzon Hall, and will remain open over to-day (Friday.) And a very
good show it is, interesting alike to the "fancy" and the novice in
matters doggy. There are terriers of every description—foxy, of course
—rough-haired, smooth-haired, and wire-haired, including the terrier
which works up his bark inside and snaps to his jaws before it has time
to issue forth. In addition to the ordinary prize list, there are a number
of special prizes (exclusive of those offered by the club) the following
gentlemen being among the donors :—Messrs. Mosenthal, Warwick
Pemberton, O. B. Gem, H. J. Clements, Samuel Boddington, Maxwell
and Cassel, Douglas Mitchell, R. H. Cartwright, F. Toomer, F. Mayhew,
A. H. Clarke, W. R. Hues, and last, but not least, Mr. James Dean,
a gentleman well and favourably known in the vicinity of Temple
Street.

1887

APRIL 25, 1925.

THE TOWN CRIER.

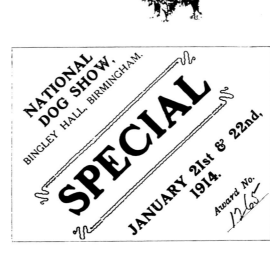

HANDSWORTH CANINE ASSOCIATION

SUCCESSFUL SHOW

LIST OF AWARDS.

The Handsworth (Birmingham
Canine Association held the second
a series of members' sanction shows
the Farcroft Hotel on Thursday eve-
ing. In all the classes there was ke
competition, especially so in t
classes for Alsatians, smooth and wi
fox terriers. The judge (Mr. J.
Shaw, of Bolton) expressed his sati
faction at the quality of the exhibi
which numbered 144. Mr. B. E. Bra
ham was an efficient steward, whil
the secretarial duties were carried o
by Mr. C. Holder. For the best dog
show, Mr. W. J. Phillips' "Tinte
Top Notcher," was awarded the fir
prize. In addition, the same exhib
secured premier honours in the class
for Airedales, Any Variety Sportin
Any Variety Terrier, and class for e
hibitors who had never gained a fir
prize in that association. Miss
Sturrock's "Salaams Wolf," exhibit
in the Alsatians Class, was awarde
first prize, whilst the best spaniel wa
that shown by Mr. J. B. Hedley. M
T. H. Day's "That's a Darlint" w
awarded the premier prize in the pupp
class. Mr. W. R. Steer's "Mounta
Con" won similar honours in th
Collies' Class.

THE NATIONAL DOG SHOW.

One of the most important coming eve
in the Midlands is the National Dog Sh
which will take place in Bingley Hall
December 8 and 9. The committee ha
provided 764 classes, including the
tional Puppy class, for which six pri
amounting to 30 guineas, will be giv
In every breed a class "Not for compe
tion" has been provided. Local classes
scheduled for the following breeds on
Bulldogs, Airedales, Wire and Smoo
Fox Terriers, Pugs, Pekingese, Poms, T
Spaniels, and Yorkshire. The entry
for each of these classes is 5s.

There are upwards of 600 special pri
including the usual challenge cups a
bowls, as in the past.

The Borzois Club and the Setter a
Pointer Club are holding their ann
shows in connection with this show, a
special classes have been provided
members of the Midland Cocker Span
Club and for members of the Brit
Alsatian Association. In the latter c
the classes will be judged by Mr. W.
Partridge on the second day.

As will be seen from our advertisem
columns, entries close on Tuesday ne
November 23.

1920

44

1. Miss Alice Whishaw's Skye terrier, Aberdeen Monarch: 1st and championship.
2. Mrs. R. Fytche's cocker spaniels, Fulmer Over, winner of two 1sts, Fulmer Peat, winner of two 1sts, two specials, and championship, and Fulmer Joanna, winner of two 1sts, two specials, and championship.
3. Mrs. J. Alastair Campbell's Brocaire Knapdale: 1st in the limit dogs for Cairn terriers.
4. Mrs. Edmunds with her winning bloodhounds, Ledburn Beau Brummell, 1st and championship, Ledburn Belinda, 1st, and Ch. Ledburn Binnacle, 1st and championship, and 1st for brace class.
5. Mr. F. L. Rayner's Fearless Vellore: 1st in puppy class for bulldogs.
6. Mr. T. W. Twyford's Ch. Type of Whitmore, 1st and championship for best dog, and Thelma of Whitmore, three 1sts and championship for best bitch, in Labrador retrievers.
7. Mrs. N. Fleming with her Cairn terriers, Speedwell Out of the West, 1st novice bitch, and Fireboy Out of the West, championship for dogs.
8. Miss M. S. Fanshaw's dachshund, Princess Dagmar: two 1sts, 2nd, four specials, and reserve championship.
9. Mrs. E. M. Morgan's Japanese spaniel, Iki-Oki: 3rd and reserve, and Mr. W. R. V. Morgan's Ugo: 2nd.
10. Mrs. Graham Williams' chow-chow, Pecknall Daphne: three 1sts, eight specials, and championship.
11. Mrs. M. Benson's pug, Ch. Dollalan, 1st and championship, making its 28th championship.

THE
BOURNVILLE WORKS MAGAZINE

Edited by W. E. COSSONS.   September, 1944

THE DOG SHOW
The Birmingham Kennel Association's Show at Rowheath attracted 334 entries, from Alsatians to Pekinese.

HOLIDAYS AT HOME
ANOTHER WAR-TIME SEASON ENDS

ANOTHER Bournville "Holidays at Home" season has been brought successfully to a conclusion and another contribution—we hope a useful one—has been made to a "Brighter Birmingham." Next year, let us hope, will see at the least the beginnings of a return to more normal holidays.

There is no need to give the whole programme in detail, but it may be mentioned that—thanks very largely to the "super summer" weather which blessed the "General"—the close of the season saw both the entertainment and the size of the crowds reach a climax—the latter possibly a record for the whole series of war-time efforts.

On August Bank Holiday there were something like 5,000 people for the Maypole and other dancing, and on the following Saturday that number was exceeded when, to finish up the season, the attractions were the Birmingham Kennel Association Dog Show and the Pipers and Highland Dancers of No. 1 Army Selection Centre.

Then there were several hundred more people at the Valley Pool, and of course the Lido was crowded almost every moment it was open.

There have been Sunday and week-night concerts by Bournville and other local Societies and by professional concert parties, and the military bands have proved as popular as ever. In addition to the favourites of last year, like the South Staffordshires, the Worcesters and the Home Guard, we have had another R.A.F. Band and that of the King's Shropshire Light Infantry, while, after the official programme ended, the King's Liverpool Regiment provided an additional Saturday afternoon's music, though unfortunately the weather did not do its part.

Dancing, of course, has been the mainstay of the programme, and for this the Black Dominoes Accordion Band has played twice a week.

Three United Churches Services have been held on Sunday evenings, conducted respectively by the Rev. R. B. Waterman, the Rev. G. E. Molesworth and Mr. C. L. Holding, and with addresses by Mr. J. C. Rock, the Rev. Noel Hutchcroft and Dr. H. G. Wood. The Salvation Army Citadel Band led community hymn-singing on another Sunday evening.

The Lido went on to draw its daily hundreds as long as the warm weather lasted, and even though no special entertainment was provided, many people—chiefly family parties—continued to find the lawns and trees of the Garden Club an attraction.

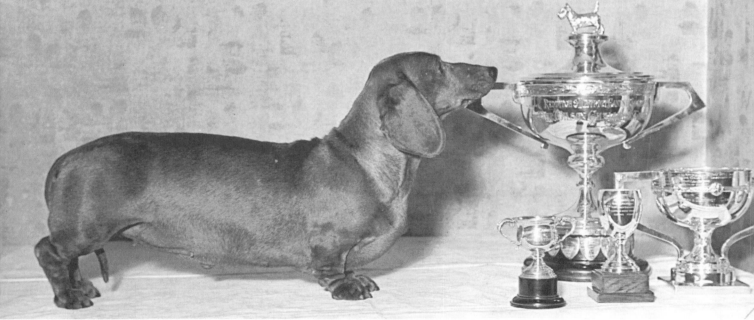

Mary Allthorpe's Dachshund, Golda, from Kings Heath, examines some of her trophies, 1950.

DOG SHOW 1945
(Staged by the "Brighter Birmingham" Canine Association),

AT CALTHORPE PARK,
SATURDAY NEXT, JULY 28.
10.30 a.m. to 7 p.m.

ADMISSION: Day Ticket 4/6, Children 2/3; from 2 p.m. 2/3, Children 1/6; from 5 p.m. 1/6

Exhibitors Sam Lowe (with Pekingese) and Mrs Perkins (with Italian Greyhound) frame well-known Judge, Tom Gasgoine, at the Birmingham and District Toy Dog Society Show, Bristol Street Schools, 1949.

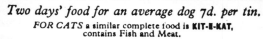

NORTHFIELD DOG SHOW.

A LEADING LOCAL EXHIBIT.

The first of the 1949 series of shows organised by Northfield Canine Association was held at the Church Hall, Northfield, on Saturday, and the continued popularity of these events was shown by the fact that 118 dogs made 342 entries. Mr. A. J. Edwards, of Elstree, had a hard afternoon's work, especially in sorting all the Smooth Terriers and the Staffs. Bull Terriers. These, along with the Cairns, were in great force.

Best in show award, a cup donated by the President, Mr. E. Gray, of Dudley, and the Sirrelstone Terrier Cup (presented by Mr. L. Bott), were won by Mr. H. Harrison, of Washwood Heath, with his Smooth Fox Terrier bitch, Attaford Avis. She was unbeaten in her six classes. The best of opposite sex award went to Mrs. I. Hooper, of Wychall Road, Northfield, with her Sealyham Meritbrook Matelot, which was only just beaten for maximum honours.

Mr. Edwards was greatly impressed by the standard of all exhibits. The Dachshunds, Corgis and Cockers did not reach their usual high standard in numbers, but the quality was good.

Photo: Lashbrook, Northfield.
Two Northfield prize-winners, Mr. A. Hooper, Wychall Road, with Meritbrook Matelot, (left) and Mr. B. Mason, Middlemore Road, with Meritbrook Meadowsweet.

The National Dog Show, organised by the Birmingham Dog Show Society (founded 1859), Bingley Hall, 1956. This particular year there were 5,862 entries, an increase of 100 on 1955.

The Birmingham National Dog Show, Bingley Hall, 1955.

Pedigree Certificate

NAME OF DOG.. K.C. REGISTRATION No..........................
BREED MINIATURE POODLE SEX BITCH COLOUR BLACK DATE OF BIRTH 24 : 1 : 58
BREEDER Mrs M. ROBERTSON BREEDER'S ADDRESS 7 SELLY AVENUE SELLY PARK B'HAM 29
OWNER.. OWNER'S ADDRESS...........................

SIRE (1)	GRAND SIRE (3)	GREAT GRAND SIRE (7)
NAME LENDREENA CHEKLO	BLUE RUSHES PIERAT 2 C.C. WINNER Reg No 85078/51	CH BRAEVAL BOLERO 10 CC WINNER
K.C. REGISTRATION No. 9155/57		GREAT GRAND DAM (8) COUNTESS OF HANNERHEAD
OWNER MRS. DYER	GRAND DAM (4) LENDREENA LADY PEPPITA Reg No 23130/55	GREAT GRAND SIRE (9) QUENTAIN PITTA PAT 27990/49
ADDRESS 37 OAKFIELD ROAD SELLY PARK B'HAM 29		GREAT GRAND DAM (10) LENDREENA SUZETTA 17397/51
DAM (2)	GRAND SIRE (5) HANSEL OF HEADSTONE Reg No 24002/52	GREAT GRAND SIRE (11) BRAEBECK TINO OF HEADSTONE
NAME BRIGETTE OF CAPELLARES		GREAT GRAND DAM (12) CANICHE BRUNETTE OF HEADSTONE
K.C. REGISTRATION No. 26757/58	GRAND DAM (6) MATINA OF MOORSTEAD Reg No 26532/53	GREAT GRAND SIRE (13) POLICHINEL OF HEADSTONE
OWNER MRS M. ROBERTSON		GREAT GRAND DAM (14) SANCROFT BROWNBERRY
ADDRESS 7 SELLY AVENUE SELLY PARK B'HAM 29		

Date 10 . 4 . 58
Signed M. E. A. Robertson
Address 7, Selly Avenue Selly Park B'ham 29.

SPILLERS LIMITED supply these Pedigree Forms as part of their service, but can accept no responsibility for any transaction involved in their use.

On their way to the Birmingham Pekingese Association's champion-ship show at Kingstanding Community Centre, Rajah and Mally pause to peek at the world with their friend Winifred Mee. The dogs belong to the Association's President, Mrs Partridge, May 1965.

WOFFLE

POOL FARM BOYS' CLUB.

10 CLASS **Exemption Show**

109 Hillmeads Rd., Kings Norton,
Birmingham 30.

20th August, 1972.

1ST Prize

Class No. 10

Exhibit No. SANDY

Across the world to see city dog show

AN international buyer from the Argentine flew to Britain this week with the sole intention of visiting the Birmingham Dog Show.

Mr. Ricardo Patalano and his son were today at Bingley Hall where the 96th Birmingham Dog Show opened.

This is the first time Mr. Patalano, a newspaper pro-prietor and owner of a Buenos Aires advertising agency, has been to Birmingham.

Mrs. Dulcie Smith, of Perry Barr, sold Mr. Patalano a Chow two years ago.

"He said today he would be looking for a bull terrier but is also interested in Pekinese," she said.

One of the show judges, Mrs. Judy de Casembroot, said to-day: "I think this show is bette rorganised than Crufts.

1968

Brigitta Hackenbeck, with Irish Wolfhound, Oliff of Eaglescrag, at the Birmingham Dog Show, Bingley Hall, November 1968.

Record entry of 7,000 for last Birmingham dog show

13.11.70.

Birmingham Post Reporter

A record entry of almost 7,000 dogs marked the last of the Birmingham Dog Show Society's national shows at Bingley Hall, Birmingham, which opened yesterday.

The show, second only to Crufts in size, is to be moved to the National Agricultural Centre at Kenilworth.

The show closes tomorrow.

Results

AFGHAN HOUNDS: Best of breed: Jasmil Twiggy of Koh-J-Noor (Mr. A. S. F. Millen, Sittingbourne). Open dog: Hajubah of Daylen (Rev. D. Ford, Burton-upon-Trent). Open bitch: Mivasht Empress (A. Doe, Arundel).
BASSET HOUNDS: Best of breed: Hobcote Folly (A. Hainsworth, Shipley). Open dog: Ch. Fredwell Veron Fawkes (Mrs J. Wells). Open bitch: Hobcote Folly.
BEAGLES: Best of breed: Forrardon Kinsman (Mrs P. Harris, Tring). Open dog Forrardon Kinsman (Mrs. P. Harris). Open bitch: Redgate Galety (J. Hall, Kenley).
BLOODHOUNDS: Best of breed: Barsheen Black Pirate (Mrs. Y. Oldman, Saul). Open dog: Barilla Perseus (Mrs. B. Bingham, Oakington). Limit and open bitch: Barnspark Dilemma (Mrs. J. Rawle, Minehead).
BORZOIS: Best of breed: Ch. Swallowcroft Reyas Ivanovich (Mr. G. Bowther, Leek). Open dog: Ch. Swallowcroft Reyas Ivanovich (Mr. G. Bowther). Open bitch: Ch. Tina of Colhugh (R. Bassett, Brighton).
DACHSHUND (long-haired): Best of breed: Ch. Endora of Murrumbidgee (Mr. A. Swan, Altrincham). Open dog: Ch. Julius of Penerley (Mrs. J. Martin, Ringwood). Open bitch: Ch. Endora of Murrumbidgee (Mr. A. Swan).
DACHSHUNDS (miniature long-haired). Best of breed: Ch. Delphik Debbnet (H. Fielding, Blackpool). Open dog: Ch. Martin Von Helzner (Mrs. J. Conneil, Padwinter).
DACHSHUNDS (smooth-haired). Best of breed: Ch. Rhinefields Diplomat (Mr. and Mrs. J. Gallop, Tixall). Open dog: Ch. Rhinefields Diplomat (Mr. and Mrs. J. Gallop). Open bitch: Timaru Tarquita (A. Hague, Guisborough).
BASENJIS. Best of breed: Ch. Topflight of Sin (D. Derry, Baldock). Open dog: Ch. Topflight of Sin (D. Berry). Limit and open bitch: Titian Star of Temki (Misses Juniper, London).
DACHSHUNDS (miniature smooth-haired): Open dog: Ch. Prince Albert of Wendlitt (J. Littmoden, Christchurch). Open bitch: Ch. Wingcrest

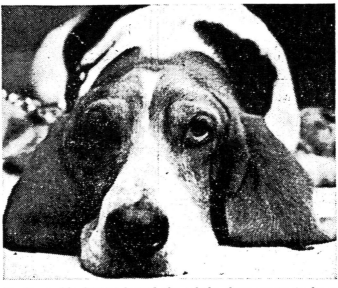

To the noble Basset hound the whole show seems to be a boring event.

Principal Girl (Mrs. M. Batteson, Sheffield).
DACHSHUNDS (wire-haired). Best of breed: Ch. Gisbourne Milton (Mrs. B. Farrand, Stockton-on-Tees). Open dog: Ch. Gisbourne Milton (Mrs. G. Farrand). Open bitch: Ch. Amplets Imperial Star (Mrs. V. Gower, Cirencester).
DACHSHUNDS (miniature wire-haired). Best of breed: Ch. Vienda Live Wire (Miss Harriman, Preston). Open dog: Silvae Enormouse (Mrs. Grosvenor Workman, Stoulton). Open bitch: Ch. Vienda Live Wire (Miss Harriman).
DEERHOUNDS. Best of breed: Ch. Amoretta of Champflower (Mrs. M. Dickinson, Taunton). Mid limit and open dog: open bitch: Ch. Amoretta of Champflower (Mrs. M. Dickinson).
ELKHOUNDS. Best of breed: Borellan Lola of Torden (Mrs. G. Harburn, Bradford). Open dog: Brann of Eskamere Mrs. A. Heward, London). Open bitch: Borellan Lola of Torden (Mrs. G. Harburn).
FINNISH SPITZ. Best of breed: Cullabine Juniper (Mrs. G. Price, Horley). Open dog: Cullabine Juniper

(Mrs. G. Price). Open bitch: Koparl Adella (Mrs. P. King, Missenden).
GREYHOUNDS. Best of breed: Cormoran Quattam Beau Brummel (G. Pearce, Falmouth). Open dog: Cormoran Quotarra Beau Brummel (G. Pearce). Open bitch: Shalfleet Swing High (Mrs. B. Odell).
IRISH WOLFHOUNDS. Best of breed: Sulhamsted Delia (Mrs. F. Nagle, Petworth). Open dog: Ch. Sulhamsted Match (Mrs. F. Nagle). Limit and open bitch: Sulhamsted Della (Mrs. F. Nagle).
RHODESIAN RIDGEBACKS. Best of breed: Ch. Saskia Bizwent (Mrs. I. Field, Bristol). Open dog: Ch. Fundu of Footpath (Mr. and Mrs. I. Woodrow, High Wycombe). Open bitch: Ch. Saskia of Bizwent (Mrs. I. Field).
WHIPPETS. Best of breed and open bitch: Ch Harque the Lark (Lady Anderson, Blandford). Open dog: Deepridge Minstrel (Miss E. M. Hawthorn, Doveridge).
IBIZIN HOUNDS: Best of breed: Eliquinto of Hardman (L. Ridyard, Bolton). Open dog or bitch: Eliquinto of Hardman.

ENGLISH TOY TERRIERS (black and tan). Best of breed: Ch. Lancer of Leospride (Mrs. L. Boud, Watford). Open dog: Ch Lancer of Leospride (Mrs. L. Boud). Open bitch: Ch. Stealaway Golden Quaker (F. Palmer, Camberley).
CHIHUAHUAS (smotho-coat). Best of breed: Maerlake Tansy (Mrs. C. Robinson, Leamington). Open dog: Kingsmere Merry Mascot (Mrs. J. Kings, Chichester). Open bitch: Ch. Stoberry Delcarchi Melinda (Mr. and Mrs. G. P. Roberts, Birmingham).
GRIFFONS BRUXELLOIS. Best of breed: Starbeck Fireking (Mrs. E. Fenn, Pulborough). Open dog: Enavant Alumchine Jolyon (Mrs. M. Forwood, Evesham). Open bitch: Chosendale Louella (Mrs. B. Rumney, Bredon).
ITALIAN GREYHOUNDS. Best of breed and open dog: Ch. Fleeting Flavius (Mrs. M. Garrish, Rudgwick). Open bitch: Fleeting Swan Song of Follysend (Mrs. M. Garrish).
JAPANESE. Best of breed and open dog: Kogato Bushi (Mrs. M. Fanthorpe, Doncaster). Open bitch: Ch. O'Kavama of Riu Gu (Mrs. E. A. Crauford, Broadway).
KING CHARLES SPANIELS: Best of breed and open dog: Royal Toby of Oakridges (Mrs. K. Parkinson, Wakefield).
MALTESE. Best of breed and open dog: Ch. Vicbrita Sebastian (Mrs. R. White, Colyford). Open bitch: Burwardsley Shot Silk (G. A. Davis, Broseley).
MINIATURE PINSCHERS. Best of breed and open dog: Torpin Herman (Mr. J. Thomas, Halifax). Open bitch: Bragan Tuly Fair (Mrs. M. Semple, Warsop).
PAPILLONS. Best of breed and open bitch: Ch Inverdon Endora (Mr. G. Henderson, Aberdeen). Open dog: Inverdon Dick Turpin (Mr. G. Henderson).
PEKINGESE. Best of breed and open dog: Ch Chuffys Charm of Changte (Mrs. R. Bull, Wakefield).
POMERANIANS. Best of breed and open dog: Ch Mosey the Menace of Vernil (L. Weinert, Cholsey). Open bitch: Fashion Lady of Aurum (Miss R. Berney, Lewes).
PUGS. Best of breed and open dog: Willapop Horatio of Elmsleigh (Mr. R. Gibson, Silverstone). Open bitch: Rydens Oh My of Babraham (Mrs. W. Young, Leatherheaed).
YORKS TERRIERS. Best of breed and open dog: Dorrit's Maestrouds Hot Toddy (Mrs. D. Baynes, Dagenham). Open bitch: Viada Vanessa (Mrs. V. Monger, Oakengates).
MINIATURE POODLES. Best of breed and open dog: Ch. Beritas Ronlyn Rockafella (Mrs. R. Gee, Manchester). Open bitch: Nairda Spring Rhapsody (Mrs. P. Harwood, Slough).
POODLES (toy). Pixiecroft Plutocrat (Mrs. D. Davies, Bournemouth). Open dog: Great Westwood Sibon Circus Jester (Mrs. S. Barratt, Chesham).

THE MIDLAND COUNTIES POODLE CLUB

SENDS WARM GREETINGS TO FRIENDS ALL OVER THE WORLD
CHAMPIONSHIP SHOW at Bingley Hall, Birmingham, Saturday 10 March 1973
Judges: Mrs Judy de Casembroot, Miniatures. Mrs Rita Price Jones, Toys. Standard judge to be announced later. All varieties with challenge certificates
Limited Show 14 July 1973   Open Show 24 November 1973
Hon Secretary: Mrs Margaret Worth, The Orchard, Glover Street, Redditch, Worcestershire. *Telephone* Redditch 63502

Winifred Branker, President of the Sutton Coldfield Dog Training Club, examines the trophies at the club's last show at Sutton Town F.C., Coles Lane, June 1974. Keeping a careful watch is Kirstie (who was owned by today's President Ena Stevenson). Their H.Q. is now in Hollyfield Road.

CITY OF BIRMINGHAM CANINE ASSOCIATION

CITY OF BIRMINGHAM CHAMPIONSHIP DOG SHOW

Perry Park, Perry Barr, Birmingham B42

**FRIDAY, 31st AUGUST &
SATURDAY, 1st SEPTEMBER, 1973**

NAZHAN MOONLIGHT SERENADE

THIRD PRIZE

CLASS   Nº   7   NO. ....

SIRHAN SHAZNAZ   JUDGE MR E H CRAVEN

RESERVE

R

Midland Counties Canine Society
520 Class Open (Benched) Show
Bingley Hall, Birmingham, B1
Saturday
27th January, 1973
Class Nº _____ 5
No. _____

Vetzyme

he Ostrich's ways are inherited
ut a Dog said, "Good grief, would you merit it —
uried bones in my time,
ut a head seems a crime,
r he might just forget where he's buried it."

                              A.D.

THEY'RE in the dog house — and happy about it. The organisers of this year's City of Birmingham Show, that is.

And it's all because of the Championship Dog Show.

Entries have reached 15,009, the most ever received for a dog show anywhere in the world.

This tremendous entry represents 8,605 different dogs in 120 different classified breeds.

A success story, then. But a story that has brought its problems.

"It was planned to house the Dog Show in 15 huge marquees, with judging taking place in 42 rings," one of the organisers said.

"But this entry has given us one of the biggest headaches we have ever had since the show was first organised by the city in 1947.

"It has meant scouring the country for additional marquees to add to the 125 that have been ordered for the whole show.

"Moreover it has meant re-organising the layout in order to accommodate them."

The Dog Show occupies more than 10 acres of the 100-acre showground.

Judges at the show come from all over the world—Finland, the United States, Japan, Holland, Germany, Eire, Italy and Sweden. 1974

51

A final brush-up for these Old English Sheepdogs in the judging ring at the Birmingham Championship Dog Show, September 1976.

Roy Qualters, of Erdington, seems to have found a winning streak with his dog, Jim, who won nine awards at the French Bulldog Club of England's 75th anniversary championships, April 1977.

At the Midland Scruffs Show any dog can have its day. Prizes are offered for the dog with the waggiest tail and even the dog the judge would most like to take home. Valerie Orr, of Great Barr, hopes that at the event at Hamstead Road, Great Barr, her Sandy will romp home with a prize, April 1977. All the fun is being organised by the League of Friends of the John Dando senior citizen's home.

Edward, the Cocker Spaniel, gets to grips with his rosette from the City of Birmingham Show, 1983. When Denise Barney decided to retire him from the show ring at Crufts, in 1991, he was given the Best Veteran Award.

Pat Bryant and Tony Woodward proudly show off Rudi after his Best in Show win at the 110th Birmingham Dog Show Society's Annual Show at Stoneleigh, May 1982. Rudi, the Rottweiler, who was bought through the small ads in a local paper, also won at Crufts.

In a competition to find the owner most like his dog Bill Pearce seems to have found his mirror-image in Emma, the Boxer. The judges agreed too, at the novelty dog show at the Harlequin, Shard End, May 1983.

Chelmsley Wood dog lover, Jean Beddows, found that it was a case of third time lucky when she entered her dog, Valda, at Crufts. The Large Munsterlander became Show Champion in Breed and here the pair look equally delighted with the award, February 1983.

Pat Farmer with the collection of rosettes won by Shani, her Bichon Frise, and Shani's dad, Aly, 1983.

Jaike, the Scottish Terrier, owned by Stan and Jean Green and winner of over twenty-one Best in Show awards in the city, 1985.

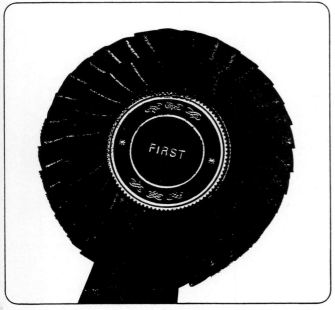

FIRST

CITY OF BIRMINGHAM CANINE ASSN.
CHAMPIONSHIP SHOW

30th & 31st AUGUST & 1st SEPTEMBER, 1985

Breed CHOW CHOW

Class No. 1260   Exhibit No. LEE-ANN

MRS SWEEN

Pedigree chum®

Judith Merrick with her Pyrenean Mountain Dog, Ziggy, at the Ladies Kennel Association Championship Show, NEC, 15th December 1985.

Joanna Brownhill, with Sheila Greening's Miniature Schnauzers, Boysie, Hattie and Tansy, at a fete at Lickey Grange School, Old Birmingham Road, 1987.

Ben, the Hungarian Komondor, wins a Best of Breed title for the fourth year running at the Birmingham Dog Show at Stoneleigh, May 1986. Nicola Snookes, from Smethwick, helps to celebrate.

Cheryl Johnson, with her Afghan, Phantom of the Opera, Perry Park, September 1987.

Joyce Lewis, of Edgbaston, with her Bedlington Terrier, Slicky, Birmingham Dog Show, Perry Park, 1989.   57

All spruced up for big dogs parade

14.5.91

HUNDREDS of working dogs competed in the final day of the world's biggest outdoor dog show held in Birmingham.

A total of 3,853 were spruced and then paraded at the National Dog Show at Perry Park, Perry Barr at the weekend.

On Saturday a total of 4,133 gun dogs and terriers competed in the 119th show organised by the Birmingham Dog Show Society.

Lhaso Apso, Ivan, Reserve Best in Show at the 1990 Acocks Green Carnival Exemption Show, relaxes at the Moseley home of his owner, Audrey Haigh, 1991.

58   *Champion dog, Beau, one of the ten Chow-Chows owned by Dawn and Paul Harris, of Northfield, March 1990.*

OPEN TO EVERYONE

KENNEL CLUB CHAMPIONSHIP SHOW

CRUFTS
CENTENARY DOG SHOW
1991

SPECIAL CENTENARY PAGEANT

AGILITY COMPETITION

BIRMINGHAM
National Exhibition Centre

JANUARY 9·10·11·12

WEDNESDAY JANUARY 9TH – WORKING DOG GROUP

THURSDAY JANUARY 10TH – TERRIER AND HOUND GROUPS

FRIDAY JANUARY 11TH – TOY AND UTILITY GROUPS

SATURDAY JANUARY 12TH – GUNDOG GROUP

OBEDIENCE, BREED AND GROUP JUDGING ALL FOUR DAYS

ADMISSION CHARGES:

ADULTS	£6
CHILDREN (3-14) AND SENIOR CITIZENS	£3

Group Rates are available

OPEN
8.30a.m. to 7.30p.m.

BIRMINGHAM

PRAMS AND PUSHCHAIRS ARE ADMITTED INTO THE HALL AT THE DISCRETION OF THE ORGANISERS.

DOGS BEING EXHIBITED MAY BE REMOVED AFTER 5PM

59

Ike, owned by Ken Humphries, helps the Lord Mayor, Councillor Bernard Zissman, launch the Crufts' ticket sales, 17th July 1990.

CENTENARY PAGEANT

The spectacular pageant produced by Charles Vance in celebration of the Crufts Centenary in 1991 has been conceived as a theatrical concept embracing one of the most exciting centuries in British history.

Crufts Dog Show

NATIONAL EXHIBITION CENTRE,
BIRMINGHAM

Liz Fox's Zola, the Hungarian Puli, winner of a challenge certificate. These unusual dogs are beginning to win agility competitions, being able to leap to a height of six feet from a standing position.

Princess Antoinette of Monaco (who runs her own animal sanctuary in the Principality) and Charles Cruft (grandson of the originator) with Anita Bellamy, of Stirchley, and her German Spitz Mitel, Jenny.

Supreme Champion, Garfield, a Clumber Spaniel, owned by Ralph Dunne, admires his trophy at the first-ever Crufts to be held in the City, 1991.

TAKING THE LEAD

MONDAY, The Daily Mail MAY 23, 1927.

GREYHOUND RACING IN BIRMINGHAM: SPECIAL "DAILY MAIL" PHOTOGRAPHS

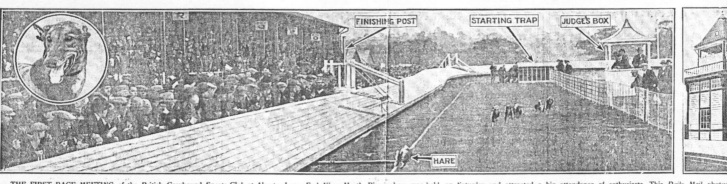

THE FIRST RACE MEETING of the British Greyhound Sports Club at Alcester Lanes End, Kings Heath, Birmingham, was held on Saturday and attracted a big attendance of enthusiasts. This *Daily Mail* photograph shows the dogs in the second race at full stretch, after the electrically propelled hare, passing the judge's box for the first time round the course, while attendants remove from the track the starting-trap from which they have just been released. In circle: Mr. R. Smith's Mission, the winner of the first race. On right: The control tower from which the electrical apparatus is worked.

Some of the first dogs to race at Hall Green preparing for the opening of the track, 24th August 1927.

Hall Green Greyhound Stadium (with Brooklands Road in the foreground), c. 1935.

63

Whippet racing comes back to Birmingham. Club secretary, Mr C. A. Stone, shows members the new ground of the Birmingham Whippet Racing Club at the rear of the College Arms, Kingstanding. The re-formed club had been out of existence since before the war, 24th April 1957.

Shanti, owned by Cheryl and Dave Johnson of Hall Green, takes off in the Afghan Races, Warwick Greyhound Track, 1986. Cheryl and Dave now own Paws 'n' Claws and Khados Kennels at Portway.

Jo Birtles, from Quinton, is one of a rare breed herself – a female in charge of a Husky team. With her are her Siberian Huskies, Lois, Koi, Mig and Arney, May 1991.

Braving the high wind! Amie and Fleur, owned by Jean Hallard, of Kings Norton, 9th June 1991. Amie had just won the racing competition at the Affenpinscher's Garden Party at Weybridge, an event won two years previously by Fleur.

CHINESE HOROSCOPE
YEAR OF THE DOG

February 10th, 1910 to January 29th, 1911
January 28th, 1922 to February 15th, 1923
February 14th, 1934 to February 3rd, 1935
February 2nd, 1946 to January 21st, 1947
February 18th, 1958 to February 7th, 1959
February 6th, 1970 to January 26th, 1971
January 25th, 1982 to February 12th, 1983
February 10th, 1994 to January 30th, 1995

FINAL MEETING

KINGS HEATH RACECOURSE

GREYHOUND RACING ASSOCIATION LTD.

WEDNESDAY, MARCH 31st, 1971

NOT SO CLEVER

Walking along a canal bank, a man idly threw a stick into the water. A stray dog plunged down the bank, slithered across the top of the water and retrieved the stick.

The performance, to the man's amazement, was repeated two or three times. Hailing a passer-by who, it transpired, knew the dog, he enquired the reason for the dog's astonishing ability to walk on water.

"Not so clever really," said the other. "He only does it that way because he can't swim."

A FEW LOCAL PERSONALITIES

(AND THEIR TWO-LEGGED FRIENDS!)

Maggie May Randle, kennel owner and well-known breeder of Pomeranians, with some of her cups, Bournville, 1936.

Much-loved actress and member of the Alexandra Theatre Repertory Company, Eileen Draycott, presents a bouquet to Mary Morse to commemorate her 80th birthday, 1954. Mrs Morse was Vice-President of the Birmingham and District Toy Dog Society.

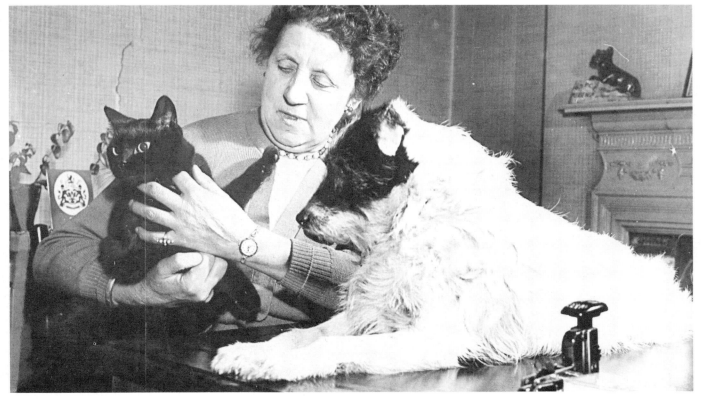

Veterinary practitioner, Marian Almond, with Binkie and her Terrier, Hudi, in her flat at the back of the RSPCA headquarters, Bristol Street, 1950. Marian was awarded the Margaret Wheatley Cross for "Her courage and humanity in conveying a number of animals to safety during an air raid at Birmingham, 20th October 1940."

Tony Hancock takes a break from filming "The Rebel" and is exercised by his rebels Charlie and Mr Brown, 1960. Appropriately, as he was born in the city, the Midlands branch of the Tony Hancock Appreciation Society is based in Birmingham.

Radio and television personality, Kenneth Horne ("Beyond Our Ken", "Round the Horne", etc.), auctions toys for the Guide Dogs for the Blind Association, John Bright Street, December 1963. Kenneth was also a director of Triplex and, at one time, owned a record shop in Pershore Road, Cotteridge.

Olive Grindey, with her Shih Tzus, 28th June 1966. Mrs Grindey is now the Secretary of the City of Birmingham Canine Association and the Birmingham Dog Show Society.

Pat Astley and his son, Gordon, with Chan, their ex-Police Alsatian, Sheldon, 1967. For several years Pat was a Continuity Announcer for ATV and appeared regularly in the children's programme "Tingha and Tucker". Gordon can be heard these days with his highly entertaining morning show, on BBC Radio WM. The three of them raised thousands of pounds for charity.

Bev Bevan, of the Electric Light Orchestra, with his Great Dane, Pongo, 1978.

Alton, with his Old English Sheepdog, Groucho, and some young helpers, just before going off to open the Birmingham Dogs' Home Summer Fete at Lightwoods Park, 20th July 1980.

Husband-and-wife team, actress Sue Hanson (Miss Diane in "Crossroads") and singer Carl Wayne, lend their support to the Birmingham Dogs' Home Open Day, 25th June 1982.

Central TV's Bob Warman (L) with his equally famous dog, Oscar, meets up with fellow newsman John Caine and some of the friends who will join them on 27th March 1983. The occasion will be a sponsored walk through Sutton Park in aid of the mental health charity, Mind.

Local pop star, Roy Wood, presents Ziggy and owner Emillie Fane with a cheque to buy four guide dogs for the blind, 18th March 1986. £4,000 was raised, in less than a year, by various events at the Bromford pub, Bromford Bridge.

Yardley MP David Gilroy-Bevan and his wife, Cynthia, found Ben darting about in the traffic at Five Ways. After rescuing him this photograph appeared in the Birmingham Mail and his owners were able to claim him. 1987.

TV comedian, Bob Carolgees, currently starring with Cilla Black in "Surprise, Surprise", first came to fame with his puppet, Spit the dog. The former Birmingham policeman's daughter, Natalie, now has her own mini Spit, January 1987.

BBC Radio WM presenter, Tony Butler, is joined by Rags, the Mongrel, as he films a light-hearted documentary on the canals, 27th July 1987.

Comedian, Malc Stent, researches his material for the charity concert, at the Crescent Theatre, in aid of the new home, May 1988.

Ex-model Toni Jay, from Sutton Coldfield, with her Yorkshire Terriers, Benjy and Biggles, February 1989.

Birmingham Dogs' Home Manager, John Goodhead, meets bearded local actor, Pat Roach, and collects a cheque for £726, raised during a sponsored jog at the Helios Health and Fitness Club, October 1990. Pat was a regular in the TV series "Auf Wiedersehn Pet" and has appeared in several films, including the Bond epic "Never Say, Never Again".

PAWS FOR ENTERTAINMENT

1926

Long complete stories of SEXTON BLAKE, the world-famous Baker Street detective, and his two assistants, TINKER and PEDRO (the bloodhound), appear each week in the UNION JACK.

JUST STARTING

"From Prisoner to President"

a thrilling New Serial by

STACEY BLAKE

UNION JACK

Every Thursday.　　　　　Price **2D.**

Buy your Copy TO-DAY!

THE HOUND OF THE BASKERVILLES

Sir Arthur Conan Doyle

1965

Brilliant new magazine designed to delight everyone who owns a pet

Barbara Woodhouse, possibly the best known trainer in the U.K. (famous for her stentorian cry "walkies"), meets David Hall and Gino at a book-signing session at the Midland Educational, Corporation Street, 22nd October 1981.

"Have you seen my dog this morning, Mr. Smith?"

"Seen him! I should think I have. He came in here, stole a leg of pork, bit me in the foot, then tripped a customer into a crate of eggs."

"Did he really? Well, I wonder if you would mind putting this 'Lost' notice in your window?"

DONALD PEERS

Donald Peers, forties and fifties singing star of radio and theatre. His most famous recording "In a Shady Nook (by a babbling brook)" is still played today.

PUNCH TO HIS DOG, A LA HAMLET.
"Toby or not Toby." 1880

Leo, the Old English Bull Terrier, was 'discovered' being taken for a walk by his owners, the Hills of Longbridge, 4th November 1986. He went on to play Bill Syke's dog in the Curnedy Musical Society's production of "Oliver" at the Palace Theatre.

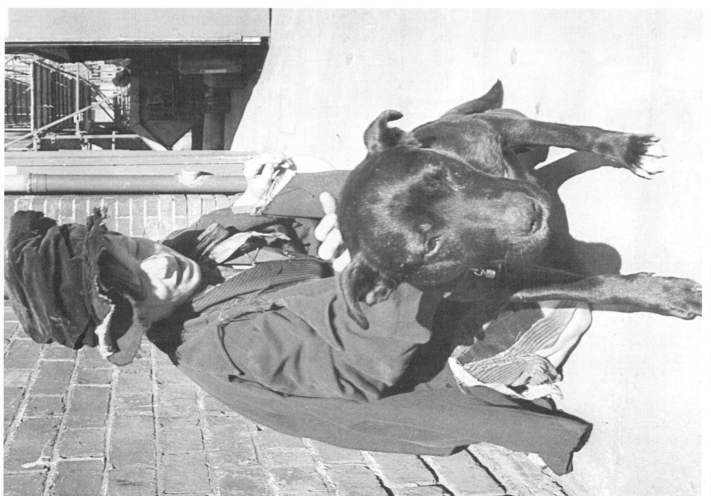

Toby, who plays "Bull's Eye" in "Oliver" at the Alexandra Theatre, with the "Artful Dodger" (Stephen Kebell), 14th September 1977. The brindle Staffordshire Bull Terrier was found in kennels but after his stage debut he had no trouble in

Comedian Bernie Winters and his partner, Schnorbitz, size-up Tommy the Cat (Wendy Williamson) during a break in rehearsals for "Dick Whittington", Alexandra Theatre, 10th December 1987. For some time Bernie was President of the St Bernard Dog Association.

George Melly, with an appropriately named "Melly" 14th July 1989. Each year the Birmingham International Jazz Festival donates a guide dog, naming the animal after a famous musician or singer.

"A Dog's Life" starring Charlie Chaplin and Edna Perviance, 1918.

The Night Cry (Warner Bros., 1926) with Rin Tin Tin

Picture Show 1934

"LUCKY DOGS"

Little Dickie Moore likes a dog with plenty of life and fun, and his black Aberdeen, Rags, is a great companion.

On the right is Richard Arlen with his Schipperke.

FILM STARS AND THEIR PETS.
MIRIAM HOPKINS   5843 C.

Son of LASSIE

THE GREAT STORY OF A SECRET SERVICE OPERATION IN THE HEART OF ENEMY-OCCUPIED NORWAY

The famous chicken-plucking scene from "Swiss Miss" where Stan Laurel, with the certain approval of Oliver Hardy, finally persuaded the St Bernard to part with his brandy, 1938. This remarkable sequence was actually shot in a single take.

Roddy McDowall, with Lassie, appearing in MGM's "Lassie Come Home", 1943. This was the first of the Lassie films and the plot centres around a poor family forced to sell its beloved dog and the animal's epic 1000 mile journey to find them.

Angela Rippon with Benson, the Basset Hound, in BBC TV's "The Animals Roadshow", 1989.

Joan Newell and Nigel Stock with Sherpa, from the BBC TV programme "Owen, MD", 1971. "Sherpa" was in fact Sheba, the Russian Samoyed, owned by Harry Bellamy, of Stirchley.

The O'Rourke family, from Selly Oak, proud owners of Border Collie, Penny, celebrate their win on the TSW programme "That's My Dog". They donated their £500 prize money to the Cinammon Trust (a boarding scheme for pets whose owners are hospitalised). John, Stuart and Beryl are with vet Eddie Straiton, host Derek Hobson (in striped tie) and "kennel maid" Louise Burton, 1987.

Robert Hardy, Christopher Timothy and Peter Davison in the BBC's "All Creatures Great and Small" (based on James Herriot's stories), 1987.

Racing manager, Simon Harris, with Flashy Tania and Flashy Madam, the dogs featured in the ITV documentary "Greyhound", Hall Green Stadium, 1989.

"WOOF"

(Central Independent Television).

Current children's series which tells the story of a boy who turns into a dog. Many of the animals were trained by the Birmingham-based Solihull Dog Training Club and neighbouring clubs.

James Ellis with Eric-the-dog (played by Tich).

Standing (L to R) Geoffrey Davies and James Cossins. Seated Ruth Madoc, Thomas Aldwinkle (as the boy who turns into Eric-the-dog) and Lisa Goddard.

Children's TV presenter, Tommy Boyd, with Tich and some cycling friends.

A DOG'S TALE.

§

1878

I'm a dog you know—perhaps you've seen me in Cow Street—I'm often there, every day, in fact. I am not one of your good-for-nothing mongrels who do nothing but cadge about; I'm a bit too knowing for that. I have studied human nature a bit, and can easily pick up a living; not easily, perhaps, for we work pretty hard some days, or rather I work hard; he does'nt do much. "He" is my mister, you know, and is blind and deaf, and all the rest of it, or, at least, he says he is. I don't say that he is'nt; oh, no! I am a trifle too knowing for that. Don't gull the public, too, that's all. We start from home about nine, and saunter up and down Cow Street all day—that is, on fine days; we don't always work on wet days, we go to a public-house. We have a splendid dodge for gulling the public, we have. I sit up and beg, and look awfully miserable, and passers-by say "poor litttle doggie," and drop a penny in the cup. I know the penny is meant for me, but, bless you, I don't get it. We keep on all day, me sitting up and he taking the pennies. Sometimes we take a lot of money; almost any day after 12 o'clock e could give you change for half-a-sovereign in coppers. One day I ounted seventeen shillings, and I wanted to go home, but "he" said ' no; lets' take a pound, because I've got company coming to-night." I stopped, of course, for I knew I should have some chicken bones, and lots of nice things.

Don't I hate those *Mail* boys! They come bawling round me until I m quite frightened. I mean to bite one of them some day.

I know lots of other fellows in our way—catch one in the dark. I know lots of other fellows in our way; not exactly our way either, because they don't sham as we do. They sell books, and eye-glasses, and pins and needles, and all the rest of it. We never take any notice of those vulgar fellows you know, because we are professionals, they are in trade—although we can't help knowing them by sight. Didn't they make a row about that fire in Digbeth the other day selling 'memory' cards, and all that you know. "He" condescended to speak to one of them one day, and asked him not to make such a noise (although I could'nt make it out quite what difference it made to him considering that he was deaf), but the vulgar fellow said 'twas no use trying to do trade now-a-days without a lot of shouting. 'Times had altered,' he said, "and folks had given up believing that 'the worst spoke in the wheel crakes most.' " I begun to like that fellow, but I hated him again a minute or two after when I heard him say for a fact—" I wish somebody would bring out a photograph of the bloke, and his missis, and the servant girl, they'd sell." I hate a man who uses such language as that. If "he" only knew I sent this should'nt I get a licking, that's all. "He " licks me awfully sometimes when there's nobody looking. That's what makes me look so miserable. I don't mind sitting up and begging only I'm afraid that if I keep on I shall wear out my tail.

K. D."

DOGS' TALES

* * *

BOY AND DOG.

An amusing scene was witnessed in Navigation Street the other day. A number of ragged urchins had been teasing a dog of rather ample proportions. Doggie stood it well for a few minutes, and then suddenly assumed the aggressive, and chased the boys. One of the most ragged of them was last in the crew, and the dog caught him up. The affrighted lad, seeing there was no means of escape, stood up against the wall, and put up his hands pitifully, saying, "It wasn't me! It wasn't me!" The idea of the lad appealing in speech to the dog caused the bystanders to burst forth into loud peals of laughter. The lad ought to thank his lucky stars that the muzzling order has not yet been revoked, or he would have been transformed into a more abject study in tatters than he then was. **1898**

Pro Bone-o Publico

TIM TALE - By C. B. POULTNEY

THERE were three of them. A large shaggy dog with a droopy expression; and two smaller dogs. And the large one had a bone. He wasn't eating it. It lay on the pavement at his feet and actually appeared to be a nuisance to him rather than a pleasure. Candidly, I think that dog was a poet. He had a dreamy, far-away expression, and he brooded over that bone as if he were trying to compose a sonnet about the thing.

The two smaller dogs obviously thought this was a silly notion. Their idea of a bone was a thing to be eaten. Quickly. They couldn't take it away by force because the drooper was larger than they were; so they got as close as they dared and dropped pointed hints.

"Now then," mumbled the poet, "where had I got to? Ah, yes. Lie there, sweet bone, on yonder stone. and —— I say," he broke off. "I do wish you two would go away. I'm busy thinking."

* * *

" JOLLY good idea," said one of the small dogs, cheerfully. "You stay here and think, and we'll take that old bone and ——"

"But it's the bone I'm thinking of." pointed out the poet, fretfully—and just then Tim arrived. (It was a bitterly cold day, for April, having come in like a lamb, was going out like frozen mutton, and Tim was dawdling along even more slowly than usual. He's like that!)

He saw the bone and advanced. Now, he has a remarkably ingratiating manner, has Tim, and the poet fell for it. "I say," he began, "you seem a sensible chap. Can't you persuade these two to go away?"

"What, these two nippers?" asked Tim. "Easy. Scoot!" He made a threatening movement, and the two retreated. "Ha!" said the droopy one. gazing after them. "That's good. Now I can —— Hi! that's mine!"

But Tim had the bone . . . I made him give it back, of course. but I bet the poet didn't keep it. He *was* so droopy.

SOME "DOGGY" PARAGRAPHS

1934

What's the queerest-looking dog you have ever seen? Undoubtedly the answer is the Griffon. Its fierce-looking, whiskered little face wears an extraordinary resemblance to Popski's, but it is no relation to that hound. On the contrary, it claims relationship with one of the aristocrats of the dog family—the Yorkshire terrier.

* * *

The least-seen dog of all is probably the huskie, that sturdy, hardy creature of the frozen north. It is invaluable as a sledge dog in the Polar regions, being admirably suited for that purpose.

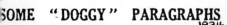

How do you like him?

* * *

For its size, the Dandie Dinmont gives the largest bark of all. It is quite a small, mouse-coloured little creature, but when it speaks everyone knows it. Incidentally, Sir Walter Scott's novel, "Guy Mannering," brought this sporting little breed into the limelight.

* * *

What's the ugliest dog? The bulldog wins this easily, but in spite of its fierce-looking appearance, it is one of the most gentle and mildest-tempered dogs you could possibly have. They're affectionate old fellows, too!

Sheila Hunt keeps a protective arm around Laddie, Harborne, 1940. The Border Collie would act as an early-warning system and alert the family to the presence of enemy bombers long before the sirens were sounded.

BOW-WOW, to-day let's shout hooray and sing a merry VE-Day lay. I don't quite know what VE may be, but it's a good thing, seems to me.

For instance, Uncle stroked my head. "It's dear young Peter Pup," he said. "Let him, I beg, have some rich treat. Peter, what would you like to eat? My slipper? Well, now, for to-day I'll hand it to you. Shake it, pray!"

So I very naturally shook it. In fact, by the time I'd finished with it you'd hardly know it *was* a slipper.

Then I went in the garden, and what happened? The gardener laid aside his hoe, and looked at me and said, "Hullo, it's my young friend, the Peter Pup. The garden's yours, mate—dig it up!"

So I dug. Good old Mr. Sandyman! When I got indoors again I met Nurse, and instead of making rude remarks about dirty faces Nurse merely laughed and said: "Well, look at Peter. I declare he's had a lovely time somewhere. Well, well, why *shouldn't* he have fun? Look, Peter, here's a luscious bun."

Oh, there's no doubt about it: this VE-Day business is a GOOD THING!
Yours doggedly,
PETER (VE-ry good) PUPPY.

Within a month Sputnik II circled the earth — with a live animal — the dog Laika, aboard.

It appeared over Birmingham where the staff at Edgbaston Observatory described it as "like a bright star" in the early hours of November 6.

It was seen for 15 minutes — the brightest thing in the sky."

Man WAS on his way to the Moon.
1957

Dumpling, the bull mastiff with a passion for pork pies, is poorly. Early diagnosis: over-eating caused by excessive hospitality from ITV personnel.

Dumpling (pedigree name Rajah of Old Oscott) lives in the pub next-door to the Television Theatre at Aston Cross. Never—not until today, at any rate—has his 147 lb. frame been beaten for pork-pies.

One night a customer challenged Dumpling that he could drink more bottles of beer than Dumpling could eat pork pies. At the end of an hour, with 11 empty bottles beside him, the customer gave up. Dumpling was still licking his lips and asking for more.

But some-one must have "doctored" the pies last night. Put beef in them or something. Ever had a pork pie hangover? From the sad look of Dumpling, don't ever, ever try it!
1956

Alive, thanks to the dog

As usual, my small daughter and I made our way to the shelter, as we did ever day at dusk, at our home in Highfield Road, Sparkhill.

My husband joined us later, after walking home from work. My husband had reinforced our shelter with concrete porch and we thought we were reasonably safe, until there were three terrific explosions.

The electric light went out at once, and we were unable to get out, as the shelter was completely covered, and we were trapped. I cannot speak too highly of the rescue people, who came from Hall Green in a matter of minutes.

They managed to dig us out, but there were three huge craters (right) and we had to remain in the shelter till day time. One crater was 38ft across, big enough to take a horse and cart.

The blast must have just missed our shelter, but next door, the people were buried, no sign of where the shelter had been. The rescue people were about to give up, when my husband heard a scratching. It was their dog. It had saved their lives.
(Mrs.) M. Hughes
Chadwick Avenue
Rednal   *2ⁿᴰ W.W.*

Inky barks at milkman — 'He's back to normal'
1970
Evening Mail Reporter

INKY, an ageing poodle, barked at the milkman today. So his owners knew there were no lasting effects from his weekend ordeal.

For when a car thief decided to take a Birmingham man's car, he either failed to notice, or did not care, that Inky was on the back seat.

The car was taken from the car park of the Scott Arms, Great Barr, where it had been parked only minutes before by Inky's owner, Mr. James Scott, of 11, Lammermoor Avenue, Great Barr.

Mr. Scott and his wife, Catherine, had just returned from a week's caravan holiday in Saundersfoot, South Wales. The couple had stopped at the shops for a few items of food —including fresh meat for Inky.

It was nearly 12 hours before the car was recovered by Warley police, several miles away in Talbot Road, Bearwood, Smethwick. Inky was taken for a walk by a policeman and then returned home.

A small Foxhound Terrier is released, after being trapped between a concrete pillar and iron bars. RSPCA Inspector Goodenough tied a rope around the bars and the axle of his car and managed to bend the bars sufficiently to release him, Dennis Road, Sparkhill, March 1958.

After a four-day absence Pip, the Corgi, was found just a half a mile from the Park View Hotel, Handsworth, where his owner was staying when he escaped. Oliver Jones and his daughter, Thelma, had hoped to exhibit him at Bingley Hall, November 1963.

The life of a model can be very boring as Omar, the Afghan Hound, finds out while posing for Elsie Collins at the Fir-Cone Festival, Bingley Hall, 15th June 1972.

Midget, the Schnauzer, and Sadie, the Dalmatian, throw a party in honour of their new Mongrel friend, Dona, at the Harborne home of their owner Beryl Romano, 20th April 1972.

METER NOT YET IN USE

ARK·O·METER
MADE BY
VENNER L.
W MALDEN

CASSIOPEIA

A parking poser . . . !

PARKING space for boats . . . or a hitching post for the ship's dog?

This "pirate" parking meter appeared overnight alongside the canal at Birmingham's Bar Basin, off Gas Street.

Businessman Mr. Sam Waller, who made the discovery, said: "I know boat moorings are a problem these days, but this is ridiculous."

Then the mystery was explained. Officials of Birmingham Public Works Department made o check of new meters being installed in Gas Street and reported: "One of our meters is missing."

Police believe vandals had uprooted it and stuck it in a convenient hole beside the basin. Later it was put back in its proper place. 1972

Five generations of the Woodpuddle family of West Highland White Terriers, relax at the home of the Ingrams, Kings Heath, November 1973.

A change of heart by Birmingham Housing Department now means that Gwen Williams can take her dog, Sherry, with her when she moves to Chelmsley Wood, next Thursday, January 1974.

Janet Baines finds herself taken for a slide by her Retrievers, Mandy, Kate, Jane and Danny, at Canwell Show, Sutton Coldfield, December 1973. This photograph, by Dennis Ruddle, was "Highly Commended" in the Rothman's British Press Photographer of the Year Awards.

Rita, the Alsatian, regularly acts as a kitten-minder at her home in South Yardley, May 1974.

Scamp, settles down in his new Harborne home with Craig, Darren and Debbie, 30th January 1974. The Clarke family adopted the dog after his original owners moved to a Council maisonette, where animals were banned.

£20,000 worth of equipment was used to try and rescue Jasper from a culvert in Birmingham but, in the end, firemen finally fished the seven-week-old puppy out in a borrowed shopping basket! 20th May 1974.

Oscar, the Miniature Black Poodle, pined when his friend Blue, the Weimaraner, disappeared from their Moseley home. Now everything is back to normal since Blue was found by two boys and returned to the Thomas house in Moseley, June 1976.

Tessa, one of the St Bernards at Batemans Green Farm, Hollywood, has a tete-a-tete with Nelson, a Miniature Shetland pony. Kenneth Beddoes and Graham Josephs eavesdrop on their conversation, 25th January 1975.

14.3.76.

"LOVE ME — love my dogs," says the girl who has had a long line of romances come to an abrupt end when her boyfriends met that fearsome foursome of Afghan hounds.

She's Janet Mills, sitting at her home in King's Norton, Birmingham, with her quartet of offenders or defenders, whatever the case may be . . . Arry, the black one, with his mother, Naz, on the left, and Sally on the right with her son, Mr. Steve, stretched out on the floor.

"They look quiet and inoffensive now, but I've lost many a boyfriend in the past because of them," said 24-year-old Janet, who is a founder member and assistant secretary of the Birmingham Afghan Hound Training Club.

Postscript: Today Janet is happily married to Derek Keates and they have a nine-year-old son, Jordan – and a trio of dogs!

Roddy, the runaway Labrador, in a single night away from home managed to overturn every dustbin in Page Lane, Great Barr. Here he seems to be showing a preference for a certain type of dog food, 6th December 1976.

93

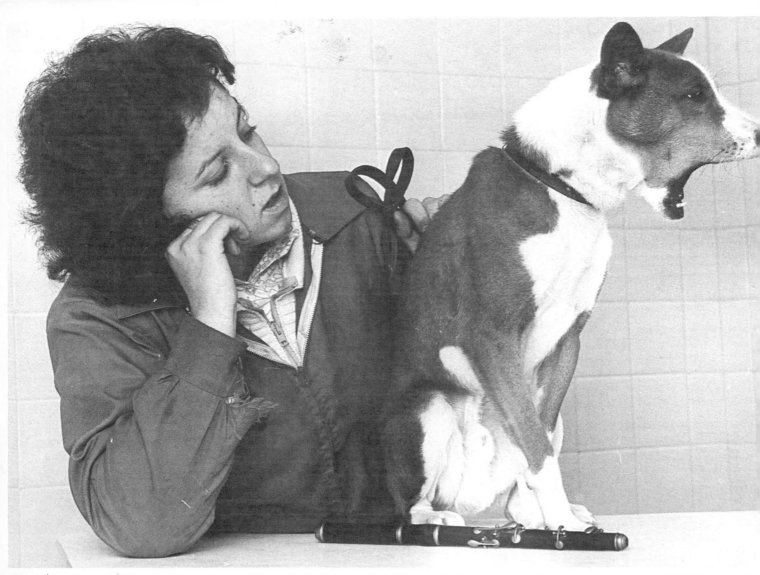

Benjy, the Basenji (African hunting dog), serenades RSPCA kennel maid Gillian Hibbert with his strange high-pitched yodel, 31st October 1976.

A DOG'S LIFE HAS ITS BRIGHTER MOMENTS — thanks to the kindhearted people who contribute each year so that the 200 strays at the Birmingham Dogs Home can have a slap-up turkey dinner with all the trimmings for Christmas. "It's mostly the pensioners who give," says Mr. John Goodhead. He and his wife, Joan, have run the Dogs Home for the past seven years, and the turkey dinner has been an annual ritual for the past five. Guests are welcome to stay as long as they need a home. Twelve 20lb. turkeys, prepared by the Goodheads on the premises, go into the doggy feast, which consists of turkey with gravy, brussels sprouts, cabbage — and chocolate drops for dessert. Do the dogs appreciate all this? "Of course they do!" affirms Mr. Goodhead. "Wouldn't you? You should see them leaping up as we come to serve them — they know a special treat's coming, and they appreciate a good meal as much as anyone."

19.12.76.

Duke, the Red Setter, was in the back of Joseph Johnson's car when it was stolen in Hillhurst Road, Harborne. By some means he managed to escape and made his way to Dudley Road, Winson Green, where he sat in the traffic outside the police station. Here he meets up with his master again, April 1977.

The car itself was found parked on double yellow lines – with a parking ticket on it!

The Jack Russell that was sold by mistake. After going missing from their home in Saltley, Sonya and Jason Bowker's Purdey was sold from a market stall for £1.50. After a great deal of sleuthing the missing pooch was returned to its rightful owners, 24th January 1978.

The National Canine Defence League has presented a citation to Great Barr Labrador, Roddy, for "Bravery in defence of his master's property despite injuries sustained", 1978. Roddy tackled would-be burglars on two different occasions.

Animal nurse, Liz Hemming, with Gandhi and his owner Clifford West. The Saluki had just won two prizes at the Birmingham Dog Show when he managed to escape, dashed into the road and was struck by a passing vehicle. However, after a six-hour search and a two-mile chase, the saga came to a satisfactory conclusion with a visit to the vet, 1978.

Guard dog, Bodger, proved to have expensive tastes when he swallowed £1,000 worth of merchandise at the Patricia Goldhill jewellery business in Hockley, January 1980. Despite a continual watch being kept on the Airedale Terrier the tiny diamonds were never discovered.

Katy makes friends with a duckling owned by her mistress, Dorothy Gallagher, Perry Barr, June 1982.

Ladywood Detective Constables, Ray Stevens and Alan Breakwell, managed to recover eight puppies stolen from their basket five days previously. In this happy picture they are re-united with Boxer mum, Toshka, 2nd September 1981.

Greyhounds, Spots of Impney and Impney Hotel, were so used to living in the peaceful atmosphere of the Chateau Impney at Droitwich that they could not adjust to the noise of life in the city. So, three months later, they and their owners, Dennis and Betty Skidmore, are on the move from their bungalow in Kings Norton, June 1982.

John Palmer, of Chelmsley Wood, has had to shave off his 17-year-old beard because his playful pet, Border Collie, Sarah, insists on tugging at his whiskers, July 1985.

Bridie, the eleven-stone English Mastiff, had the rescue services out in force when she fell through the ice in Redhouse Park, Great Barr. Tiring of several rescue attempts she eventually managed to slither across the frozen lake of her own accord, much to the relief of Hilary Clarke, February 1983.

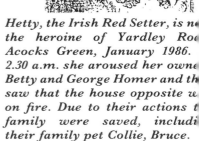

Hetty, the Irish Red Setter, is n[e] the heroine of Yardley Ro[od] Acocks Green, January 1986. 2.30 a.m. she aroused her own[e] Betty and George Homer and th[ey] saw that the house opposite w[as] on fire. Due to their actions t[he] family were saved, includi[ng] their family pet Collie, Bruce.

St Germain Brownie Pack, from Edgbaston, by collecting milk bottle tops and silver foil have managed to provide "eyes" for two blind people. In recognition of their efforts they were presented with photographs of the dogs. Special guest, Spangle, helps to mark the occasion, November 1984.

party of dogs and handlers from the West Midlands Police Force who visited the children's ward at Dudley Road Hospital, stops to chat with Adrian Leek, of Winson Green, and nurse Esther Riches, 21st April 1987.

Tom Woodall and Laddie, are convalescing, after double cardio thoracic operations, June 1987. Tom had heart surgery at the Queen Elizabeth Hospital and Laddie was saved after swallowing a large pebble.

Barbara Boscott's Mongrel, Susie, enjoys a game of football even at the age of 14. Here she limbers-up, in Bournville, with a stance that would do justice to any sporting personality! July 1985.

Stephen Shanley re-united with Beauty once again, 14th November 1988. The terrier disappeared on Bonfire Night after being frightened by fireworks in Hall Green.

Mandy, the Golden Retriever, is once again a mobile member of the canine fraternity, June 1989. After a problem with her back hips the future looked very bleak, until her owner, Andre Heathcote, had a custom-built wheelchair designed and manufactured for her in Birmingham.

Tarsem and Hardeep Kundi, with their children and cross-Collie, Prince, July 1991. Mr Kundi's father fell in love with Prince when he visited the Birmingham Dogs' Home in 1986 and took him back to their home in Moseley, where he soon became a much-loved member of the family.

Karen and Mhairi Laing, with their cross-Collies, Millie and Peggy, July 1991. The dogs were rescued after being left abandoned in a hole in the ground. They now live happily, with the family, in Selly Park.

Every night at about 9.30 p.m. Caly, the Japanese Akita, would ask to go out into the garden. Mystified her owner, Irene Hasell, followed her one evening and both of them stood and watched as a vixen played with her cubs. Sutton Coldfield, 1991.

SUNDAY MORNINGS, No. 4,

WILL APPEAR IN NEXT WEEK'S ISSUE.

SUBJECT—THE SWEDENBORGIANS AT WRETHAM ROAD, HANDS-WORTH, AND THE REV. R. R. ROGERS,

---

The Advertisement Office for the "DART" is now at MR. KIRK'S GENERAL ADVERTISING AGENCY, 82, New Street, Birmingham. The "DART" Publishing Office is situated in Fire Office Passage, New Street, and is open only from 2 30 to 7 on Friday. Papers are always on Sale at Willey's and Smith's, Union Street.

On prepayment of 3s. 3d. a copy of the *Dart* will be posted every week for six months, to any address in the United Kingdom. P.O. Orders and orders for Copies of the *Dart* to be addressed to the Publisher, *Dart* Office, Fire Office Passage, New Street, Birmingham.

Advertisements received at 82, New Street, for the *Dart* up to Thursday at noon. Tariff, Sixpence per line.

Single copies of the *Dart* may be had at 82, New Street.

A JOURNAL OF SENSE AND SATIRE.

Saturday, November 24, 1877.

THE RABIES IN MEN AND DOGS.

BIRMINGHAM, we are told, is about to follow in the wake of Liverpool and other large towns, and organise a crusade against homeless dogs. It is somewhat instructive that just at the very time when prizes are being awarded to boys and girls for the composition of commonplaces treating of kindness to dumb animals; just when Miss Kenrick's heart is filled with gratitude at the success of her scheme for turning a boy's nature inside out, Major Bond appears in the field as the inexorable enemy of homeless dogs. The spectacle of a homeless creature, whether man, woman, or child, usually touches a sympathetic chord in the most stolid heart, but somehow or another, when a homeless dog is in question, the only chord awakened is a whip-cord. The homeless dog is chased, stoned, and savaged, but the species seem to thrive nevertheless, and all the efforts of police establishments totally fail to clear the streets of a most interesting and sagacious being.

1.12.1877

WHAT WE HEAR.

That the homeless dogs of St. Martin's Ward met in secret conclave last Saturday evening, and unanimously passed a vote of thanks to the *Dart*.

That they gave an order for 1,000 copies of last week's number.

That every dog present at the meeting agreed to become a subscriber.

That great satisfaction was experienced at the number of happy dogs that have already fallen into the hands of the police.

That of the two hundred dogs captured only 15 belonged to the homeless section of canine society.

That four of these had broken legs and could not run when chased.

That three were blind and toothless.

That five were harmless lunatics.

That the remaining three or four were dogs whose deaths were not worth regretting.

That as a canine workhouse does not exist, Major Bond's crusade will assist nature in clearing out the blind and the lame.

DOGGIE MIXTURE

Dog Muzzling and Persecution.

AN honoured correspondent writes :—" I am greatly distressed to hear that the B— of Agriculture is being urged by a land-owning gentleman to have the dog — raised to one guinea, which, if carried out, will mean the cruel destruction — thousands of faithful animals, which the poorer classes will not be able — longer to afford to keep. Often I have had poor women come with tears in their — to ask help towards paying the tax, as 7s. 6d. was too much, and they could not — to destroy their pets, oftentime a sorely-needed guardian and protection to many a — woman or feeble person. The gentleman responsible for this suggestion urges in sup— that he has had sheep worried by sheep-dogs. Would it not be more equitable to — a larger tax on sheep dogs, and not fine the whole dog-owning community throug— the country!"

We quite agree with our correspondent. It will never do to place the owner — of a canine friend out of the reach of many poor people, to whom an honest — represents their total asset in loyal earthly friendship.

1896

DOG LICENCE		WQ 47196
(NOT TRANSFERABLE)		

Full Christian Names ....

and Surname ....
(IN BLOCK LETTERS)
Full Postal Address ....

....

is hereby authorised to keep **ONE DOG** in Great Britain, from the *date hereof* until and

including the *last day of* JAN 87 .... *next following;* the sum of

THIRTY-SEVEN PENCE having been paid for this Licence.

Granted at 2 hours 24 minutes............m. o'clock at the place and

on the date indicated in the issuing office stamp

by ....

NOTICE.—Any permanent change of address should be notified to the appropriate District or Island Council.

Penalty for refusing to show this Licence to any duly authorised Officer, or Police Constable, or fo— keeping a dog above 6 months old without Licence, £10

*Insert month preceeding the month of issue of the Licence.   SEE NOTES OVERLEAF

The dog licence system, which came into being in 187— lasted for 110 years and remained at 7s/6d (or 37p) unt— the end.

Olive, Evelyn and Lilian Best with their Curly-Coated Retriever, Bob, Winson Green, 1912.

1927

HARK ! hark ! the dogs do bark !
    Beggars are coming to town :
Some in rags, and some in jags,
    And some in velvet gown.

ADVOCATUS ANGELI

YOU call him rogue—it may be so ;
    Betrayer of a confidence ;
A lukewarm friend ; a coward foe ;
    A stranger to the moral sense.
All this and more : the charges grow,
    And others share your vehemence.

All true, perhaps ; but this I know :
    That when he reaches home at night,
His dog is frantic with delight,
    And licks his hand, and looks at him
With eyes that make his own eyes dim.

1929

Yesterday and To-day.

CAN there be anyone who knew Birmingham's Market Hall in childhood days
who does not still regard the old building with affectionate remembrance, as
preserving within its grey walls memories of a half-forgotten youth ?

The annual visit to the Market Hall on the Saturday before Christmas stands
prominently out of a haze of childhood memories. The Market Hall was invariably the
[fir]st ; perhaps it was nearest to the tram-route, perhaps it was first in our affections.
[As] we entered this wonderland we lingered in the Bull Ring among the flowers and

MARKET HALL PUPPIES.   1935

...ens, clutching warm pennies in sticky hands, undecided whether or not to succumb to
...[p]ersuasive oratory of the toy vendors who thronged the hill. We remember the
...[attracti]on of weighted celluloid toys, affectionately known as " kellys," and fragile metal
... which performed amazing feats on bicycles, using a dinner plate as track, which
...[hel]d the more substantial treasures within the hall.

1940

Tramp—"Could you give a poor
fellow a bite?"
Housewife—"I don't bite myself,
but I'll call the dog."

New Year's Eve Dance at the Golden Eagle, Hill Street, in aid of the Birmingham Kennel Association, c. 1951.

Lesley Reeves, of Lozells, with Buster, the Boxer, 1954

Janet Sharpe, of Greet, with her Papillon, 14th November 1967.

Edna Legg, of Acocks Green, enjoys the July sunshine with one of her Elkhounds, Falda, 1966.

Dog that went absent without leave is on the mat again

Evening Mail Reporter

ROSTI the dachshund went absent without leave from the garden of his owner's shop at West Bromwich.

He set off as fast as his three-inch long legs would take him.

Rosti waddled through Smethwick, Warley and Oldbury.

And when people saw advertisements in the "Evening Mail" appealing for information about the dog, telephone calls to the owners, Mr. and Mrs. H. P. Samuel, began to pour in.

Mr. and Mrs. Samuel have a jewellers shop at West Bromwich. But they live at Augustus Road, Edgbaston.

Disappeared

And it looked as if Rosti was en route for their home.

People tried to help. But the dog was too keen on his marathon walk to be detained.

As Mr. Samuel, received calls, he went out to the spot to track down his pet. But by the time Mr. Samuel got to each place his pet had disappeared again.

Fourteen days and 14 miles since Rosti went away, he arrived outside his master's flat.

Average speed 73 yards per hour.

Course

Mrs. Samuel said today: "From the telephone calls we received we were almost able to plot Rosti's course, but despite going out in the car every time we received a call, we never saw him until he turned up on the door mat.

"He was tired, and thin, but soon recovered after a wash and a rest." 1968

A very small boy was trying to lead a big St. Bernard up the road.

"Where are you going to take that dog, my little man?" inquired a passer-by.

"I — I'm going to see where — where he wants to go first," was the breathless reply.

Susan and Tracey Harper, from Great Barr, enjoy the snow with Sheba their St Bernard, 30th December 1968.

National Dog Show Dinner, Midland Hotel, 19

Olive and Owen Grindey (assistant secretary and secretary) at the dinner to mark the 30th annual show of the Birmingham Canine Association, St John's Hotel, 7th September 1977. Mr Grindey had been secretary since the show first began.

Cilla, the Bearded Collie and Sheba, the Rottweiler, take the air at Elmdon Park with Mar Jeys, 1970.

This tiny one-eyed Toy Poodle, with his mistress, Sheila Snook, is the aptly-named General Moshe, after the famous Israeli Defence Minister, Sparkhill, November 1973.

Police couple, June and Malcolm McCutcheon, enjoy off-duty moments with Bella, their Bearded Collie, Yardley Wood, 1975.

An unusual trio, Jenny, Lucy and Emma, pause with their owner Jackie Hill, from Selly Park, during one of their regular walks around Cannon Hill Park, New Year's Day, 1986.

PRO-DOGS GOLD MEDAL AWARD
PET OF THE YEAR
The 1990 Award
BUSTER

Andy Lloyd, Captain of Warwickshire County Cricket Club, in his Benefit Year, with his retired racing Greyhound, Dora, 1990.

Buster won his award for helping to foil an armed robbery on a post office van in Weston Lane, Tyseley.

Pro-Dogs is a National Charity, founded in 1976 by Lesley Scott-Ordish (who was born in Acocks Green) to improve recognition of dogs for the benefit of people. In 1983 Pets as Therapy (PAT) was formed as a visiting scheme to hospitals, homes for the elderly and other institutions.

Muriel Venables, with Bart and Bramble, 1990. The dogs are both ancestors of Max, who was brought to Alum Rock by Harry and Muriel Venables and was the first Briard in the area. He went on to win many prizes.

"The Magical Martyns", Celia and Kevin, with their Yorkshire Terrier, Pip, 1991.

Dogs' Home Euro moves

Birmingham Dogs' Home is putting a firm paw forward into Europe for 1992.

It has already established links with the city's twins — Lyon, Frankfurt and Milan — to increase awareness of the responsibilities of dog ownership.

"OUR GRAND FATHERS DRANK IT"

CADBURY'S COCOA

THE OLDEST AND STILL THE BEST
ABSOLUTELY PURE COCOA.

FRY'S COCOA
& Milk Chocolate

"UNAPPROACHABLE"

Fry's MILK Chocolate

& PURE CONCENTRATED COCOA

GOING BY LEAPS & BOUNDS.

Cadbury
means quality

BOURNVILLE — THE FACTORY IN A GARDEN

ACKNOWLEDGEMENTS

(For providing photographs, for encouragement and numerous other favours)

Mary Allthorpe; Gordon Astley; Pat Astley; Rebecca Aston; Denise Barney; BBC; Harry Bellamy; Bev Bevan; David and Cynthia Gilroy-Bevan; Deva Singh Bhogal; Birmingham City Council, Dept. of Planning and Architecture; Birmingham City Council, Environmental Services Dept.; The Birmingham Dogs' Home; The Birmingham Post and Mail Ltd.; Jo Birtles; Yvette Braddock; Cadbury Ltd., Archives Dept.; Dave Carpenter; Central Independent Television plc (Birmingham); Chafirlock Poodle Parlour; Ron and Miriam Clay; John and Chris Clayton; Stuart Cordon; David Dalton; Janet Dance; Shirley Dillon; Dogs for the Disabled; Dog World; Gill du Cros; Pat Farmer; Gillian Flower; Liz Fox; Dave Freeman; John Goodhead; Reg Gower; Paula Greaves; Stan and Jean Green; Sheila Greening; Barry Griffiths; Olive Grindey; Margo Hackney; Audrey Haigh; Hall Green Stadium; Jean Hallard; Tony Hancock Appreciation Society, Midlands Branch; Handsworth Historical Society; Clive Hardy; Judy Harper; Paul and Dawn Harris; Irene Hasell; Anthony Head; Roy and Dot Holmes; George and Betty Homer; Roger Hooper; Anne Jennings; Christopher Jennings; Sid and Mary Jeys; Dave and Cheryl Johnson; Derek and Janet Keates; The Kennel Club; Tarsem Singh Kundi; Karen and Mhairi Laing; Gareth Lewis; Joyce Lewis; The Lord Mayor's Parlour; Louise Dyson Model Agency; Kevin and Celia Martyn; Jayne Minchella; Mr Disk; Dave Mitty; Norman Monk; Dennis Moore; Mary Moss; The National Canine Defence League; Beryl O'Rourke; Pat Dogs; PDSA: Diane Pearce; Petsearch; Gordon Price; Pro Dogs; Eric and Dorothy Reeves; Mary Robertson; Shirley Robinson; Beryl Romano; Warwick Round; Jim Simpson; Keith Smart; Charles and Kath Smee; Geoff and Diane Smith; Marcia Smith; Solihull Dog Training Club; Sutton Coldfield Dog Training Club; Barry Tomlin; Muriel Venables; Ron Walton; Warwickshire County Cricket Club; The Weather Dept. Ltd.; Paul Wedgbury; Weintraub Film Library; Wendy Wood; West Heath Pet Stores; Joan Wilkes.

Please forgive any possible omissions. Every effort has been made to include all organisations and individuals involved in the book.

Au revoir – from Irene Hasell's Pugs, Havoc and his dad, Oscar.

111

ALTON'S BOOKS – SO FAR!

"BIRMINGHAM REMEMBERED"
"MEMORIES OF BIRMINGHAM"
"BIRMINGHAM AT WAR VOL 1"
"BIRMINGHAM AT WAR VOL 2"
"DOGS IN BIRMINGHAM"
"JOE RUSSELL'S SMETHWICK"
"THE BLACK COUNTRY AT WAR"
"MEMORIES OF THE BLACK COUNTRY"
"MEMORIES OF WOLVERHAMPTON"
"MEMORIES OF SHREWSBURY"
"MEMORIES OF WALSALL"
"MEMORIES OF DUDLEY"
"MEMORIES OF WEST BROMWICH"
"MEMORIES OF COVENTRY"
"COVENTRY: A CENTURY OF NEWS"
"COVENTRY AT WAR"
"ALTON DOUGLAS'S CELEBRITY RECIPES"
"ALTON DOUGLAS'S KNOW YOUR PLACE"

Contact leading booksellers

or

For **ORDER FORM** please write to:

Alton Douglas,
c/o Brewin Books,
Doric House,
Church Street,
Studley,
Warwickshire B80 7LG